infrastructural monument

MIT center
for advanced
urbanism

infrastructural
monument

princeton
architectural
press, new york

Infrastructural Monument

With contributions from:
Stan Allen
Pierre Bélanger
Lorena Bello Gomez
Eran Ben-Joseph
Don Briggs
Stephen Crosby
Alexander D'Hooghe
Jo Guldi
Alex Klatskin
Christopher Lee
Robert Levit
James L. Oberstar
Henk Ovink
Stephen Ramos
Adèle Naudé Santos
Roger Sherman
Marcel Smets
Malcolm Smith
Nader Tehrani
Petra Todorovich Messick
Cino Zucchi

Special thanks to:
Celina Balderas Guzman
Alan Berger
Sara Brown
Alexander D'Hooghe
Irene Hwang
Fadi Masoud
Philam Nguyen
Prudence Robinson
Yaacov Ruthenberg
Hope Stege
Mariel Villeré

Princeton Architectural Press, New York
MIT Center for Advanced Urbanism

Published by
Princeton Architectural Press
37 East Seventh Street
New York, New York 10003
www.papress.com

© 2016 Princeton Architectural Press
All rights reserved
Printed and bound in China
19 18 17 16 4 3 2 1 First edition

MIT Center for Advanced Urbanism
For more information, please visit:
http://cau.mit.edu

Massachusetts Institute of Technology
School of Architecture + Planning
77 Massachusetts Avenue
Cambridge, MA 02139–4307

No part of this book may be used or reproduced in any
manner without written permission from the publisher,
except in the context of reviews.

Every reasonable attempt has been made to identify
owners of copyright. Errors or omissions will be corrected
in subsequent editions.

Editor: Meredith Baber
Assistant Editor: Marielle Suba
Designers: Neil Donnelly and Sean Yendrys

Special thanks to: Nicola Bednarek Brower,
Janet Behning, Erin Cain, Tom Cho, Barbara Darko,
Benjamin English, Jan Cigliano Hartman, Jan Haux,
Lia Hunt, Mia Johnson, Valerie Kamen, Stephanie Leke,
Diane Levinson, Jennifer Lippert, Sara McKay,
Jaime Nelson, Rob Shaeffer, Sara Stemen,
Kaymar Thomas, Paul Wagner, Joseph Weston,
and Janet Wong of Princeton Architectural Press
— Kevin C. Lippert, publisher

Library of Congress Cataloging-in-Publication Data
ISBN 978-1-61689-420-7

Preface

This book summarizes the first conference organized by MIT's new Center for Advanced Urbanism (CAU) around its first biennial theme—infrastructure.

The spring 2013 conference, Infrastructural Monument, addressed the potential to leverage infrastructure design beyond the realm of transportation of goods and labor into the realm of culture, public space, architecture, and landscape form. At a time of increasing societal fragmentation, infrastructural spaces related to transportation constitute the last veritable common space shared by the multitude. These spaces stage us. Four panels addressed future paths for infrastructure design; each panel included a designer, a developer, a policy expert, and a scholar, in order to interlock vocabularies of design, history, implementation, cost, and consequences. This volume captures the conference proceedings on this topic. The spring 2013 conference also featured a sculpture commissioned by the CAU in memory of Manuel de Solà-Morales, who had passed away a few months before the conference. Solà-Morales was an urban planner, architect, and especially an infrastructural designer, with a practice in Barcelona and an important influence on many urbanists worldwide.

The CAU's core mission includes innovative research and design for urgent global problems concerning urbanization. Its areas of work include Climate Adaptation + Urbanism, Health + Urbanism, Global + Urbanism, and Technology + Urbanism. In addition, the CAU builds a community of experts, cities, and organizations that is committed to addressing these challenges. The members of the CAU also contribute to the curricula and education on urbanism, through both design and research, at MIT. Regular publications and conferences are important endeavors that share with the public lessons we have learned through our various projects.

We hope you will enjoy these proceedings, as they are the first of a series. Our biggest aspiration is to contribute to a more intelligent and ambitious design culture for our cities worldwide.

Introduction:
Why a Center for Advanced Urbanism at MIT?

Adèle Naudé Santos
Dean of the School of Architecture + Planning, MIT

For many years faculty members from the Department of Urban Studies and Planning, as well as the urbanism faculty in the Department of Architecture at MIT, have held joint workshops and studios investigating urban problems manifested in different global contexts. Many of these challenges came as invitations to help cities and towns with envisioning exercises for their futures. More recently, these teach-

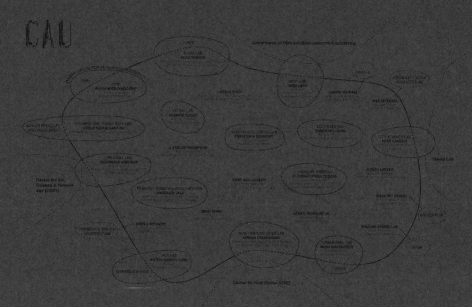

ing and learning exercises have become research projects as new urban challenges required greater analytical depth. It became clear that the MIT School of Architecture + Planning had both the interest and faculty to engage in serious research into the new challenges facing our urban futures, and the ability to broaden our expertise by collaborating with other faculty at MIT. The development of a new Center of Advanced Urbanism (CAU) was the logical outcome of this long history of faculty collaboration. Today the CAU includes faculty from research groups across MIT and has become the locus of interdisciplinary research within the school, including the Media Lab. Graduate students from urban planning and architecture have the opportunity to work with faculty on challenging projects. Through probing conferences and published research outcomes, we intend to create new theoretical frameworks and methodologies appropriate for an urbanism of our time.

Fostering collaboration between faculty and labs that are affiliated with the Center for Advanced Urbanism is one of the core missions of the CAU. (Kobi Ruthenberg, 2013)

Eran Ben-Joseph
Professor and head of the Department of Urban Studies and Planning, MIT

The future of urbanism will look nothing like it did in the past. Given the rapid pace of environmental change and resource depletion, shifting patterns of urban growth and regional development, and the transformative potential of new techniques and technologies, urban planners and designers must be prepared to revisit, rethink, revise—and at times completely reject and reinvent—our historical models of city, form, and function.

For precisely these reasons, I was pleased to work with Dean Santos and my colleagues in the School of Architecture + Planning to establish the first-ever Center

for Advanced Urbanism, a new collaborative research space at MIT. Bringing together all the relevant disciplines and approaches—architecture, planning, and development; urbanism, engineering, and ecology design; nature, science, culture, and technology—we are creating a remarkable center of exploration and excellence. From this nexus of innovation, MIT will launch the designs, methodologies, and techniques that will shape—and in fact, invent—a new urban future for the planet.

As the following pages demonstrate, the efforts of the CAU have already begun to bear fruit: Infrastructural Monument represents a bold first step in inventing the future of urbanism. I encourage you to keep watching and expect more big things.

Model of an ideal factory infrastructure layout as a flexible container for civic occupation, made for CAU exhibition about urban reuse of industrial infrastructures at the Shenzhen Value Factory during the Hong Kong–Shenzhen Urbanism Biennale, winter 2013–2014. Design and production: Kobi Ruthenberg and Alexander D'Hooghe (Mathjis Labadie, 2013)

Nader Tehrani
Professor and head of the Department of Architecture, MIT

The Center of Advanced Urbanism has been launched at MIT as one of the most potent research platforms that is not only engaging the School of Architecture + Planning, Department of Urban Studies and Planning, and the Media Lab, where its main protagonists are affiliated, but also beyond, in the faculty of the School of Engineering, the Sloan School of Management, and a variety of other departments that are looking at the developing landscape of urbanism, in its many formations and cultural variations, on a global scale. Recognizing that there is a wealth of history behind urban-design thinking, the CAU is also conscious that the very techniques and modes of inquiry associated with urban design are culturally and historically determined, making many of them unable to attend to the scale of changes that are occurring in the world today. Global warming, transnational economic recession, war and mass migration, ecological footprints across borders, and urban resilience—all themes that concern both the academic and practical arena of urban studies—are all poised to be reconsidered through the lens of a speed of development and territorial scale that is historically unprecedented. For example, cultures beyond the North American sphere, in Asia, Africa, and South America, are developing at a magnitude that is challenging an intellectual labor force that is often unable to keep up with the pace at which cities are growing, damaging the environment, and creating unsustainable urban realms. The various research laboratories within the MIT community are taking on these charged questions in both academic settings as well as workshops in the field, addressing case studies as a means to expand the intellectual grounds on which we currently understand disciplinary boundaries. Most importantly, the CAU is dedicated to bridging the gap between theory and practice and to understanding the precise material, spatial, and formal ramifications of the research underway. It is with these aims that the work of the CAU, by expanding the medium of urbanism, is broadening its reach to a critical realm.

1
transportation infrastructure as our commons

(an introduction to the conference)

alexander d'hooghe

Transportation Infrastructure as Our Commons

Alexander D'Hooghe
Associate professor and director,
Center for Advanced Urbanism

Fig. 1

Infrastructural Monument
conference, 2013
(Judith Daniels, 2013)

There exists a remarkable consensus that American cities are underperforming globally in terms of competitive state-of-the-art infrastructure. Yes, our roads need repair and our mass transit systems need capital improvements. However, the sense of malaise goes far beyond these obvious needs. The organization of this conference is premised on the understanding that the dissatisfaction with existing systems is primarily rooted in a sense of cultural impoverishment. Culture, in a quick sketch, is the sphere of expressions, direct but often sublimated and articulated through mutually agreed conventions—visual, acoustic, and otherwise—that appear when individuals or groups wish to communicate their achievements and anxieties to each other. Culture there-

fore requires, at its most basic level, a common space for these expressions to be articulated and received. Common spaces act as stages of ongoing expressive plays for any and all of us—the actors. Importantly, these stages themselves also have a form and an expression. The compound package reflects who we are not just as individuals but also as a society. We don't seem to like what is being reflected back to us.

Our common spaces are the infrastructures used by the multitude. For many East Coast cities, these include ragged highways, fraying bridges, old mass-transit cars and stations, and airports from the 1970s. Engineers and planners designed these with a single use in mind that did not include an awareness of their roles as the sole remaining physical "common" of society. While designed to connect, many of them engender a sense of discontinuity from the surrounding world. Once a citizen is in them, they are disconnected from an understanding of the physical environment beyond the infrastructural object in which they find themself. Secaucus Junction, just west of Manhattan, provides a brilliant example of this connected discontinuity. A junction of twelve different mass-transit lines, the station itself is an almost hermetically enclosed concrete box that offers no connection to the world around the station, and vice versa.

Any amalgamation of the emotional subtexts of press reports on the state of our infrastructure demonstrates a profound disillusion. Our infrastructure commons does not reflect who we think we are, let alone who we want to be, as a society. Mostly, they convey a sense of exhaustion and depletion of their cultural role, bereaving the multitude of its cultural commons.

Perhaps counterintuitively, design cannot introduce this cultural dimension if it is only conceived of as a form of decoration—adding a few big screens, brighter materials, a few trees, and better lighting. Design cannot be conceived of as an afterthought or ornament, something done after the transportation engineers and planners have done their homework and established routes, mostly on narrow cost and functionality considerations, mixed with the mitigation of stakeholder indignation. A transportation infrastructure as a cultural commons must be wired for a diversity of users (commoners) not only to enable their access but in fact attract them and ideally make their passage part of a regular routine. Both Christopher Lee and Stan Allen discuss the larger role of infrastructure in everyday routines in their entries and projects.

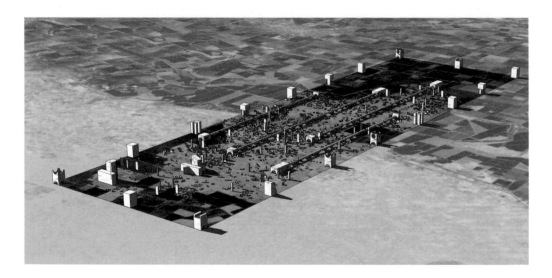

Developing an actual commons at certain junctions requires an understanding of the reasons our infrastructure production system is currently wired for failure. As Pierre Bélanger pointed out, postwar infrastructure planning was driven mostly by a series of single functionalities. Interstate highways, for instance, organize traffic in one specific direction for one type of mobility, hampering or disconnecting more local flows. Monofunctional infrastructures, by definition, rely on single modes of transportation and exclude other uses from sharing the space. For that reason, they diametrically oppose the notion of transportation infrastructure as a cultural commons. Any historical commons was legally defined by the fact that it was accessible to commoners, providing functionalities that would draw them in. A commons requires enabling the presence of a plurality of different users. An infrastructure commons project must begin by investing in multimodal transportation infrastructure. One could pursue this approach along several lines. One is to upgrade existing transportation

Fig. 2   Drawing of an ideal city based   concept of autonomy (Aristodimos
                 on Cornelius Castoriadis's   Komninos, 2012)

lines by making them multitask, multiuser, and potentially, intelligent. Pending changes in automobile technology (self-driving cars, no-exhaust cars, advanced forms of pooling) allow for the rethinking of the roadway itself. These changes are not far away—they are upon us. As a result, roadway sections can incorporate room for other uses. Another pursuit involves reactivating currently underused or obsolete transportation lines, whether railroad rights-of-way or over-designed roadway sections. Finally, developing the centralizing potential of junctions or intersections between different modes of transportation may have the most far-reaching consequences.

Multimodal stations serve more diverse constituencies, user groups, and traffic modes. Users transfer between different vehicular capsules and, during the time of that transfer, activate a common space. Multimodal stations, as Marcel Smets

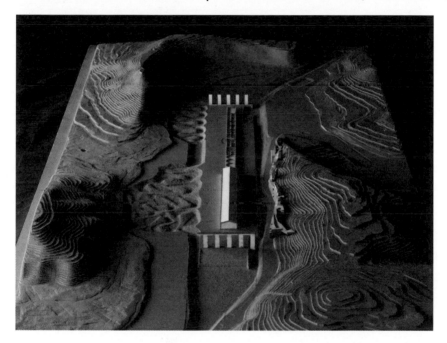

explains, take advantage of the intersection of existing infrastructure systems to exploit their capacity to serve wider audiences and offer ways to route traffic and build in redundancies. The conference proceedings present contributions from speakers that discuss both multimodal stations, and upgraded existing infraline elements in more detail.

If multimodalization and multitasking of existing lines and junctions is a first critical step toward an infrastructure commons, then bundling transportation infrastructure with other types of infrastructures would constitute a second important step toward a cultural commons. Our most successful and loved infrastructure projects in history—the parkway system, Frederick Law Olmsted's Central Park (New York)

Fig. 3   Model of a new island in the   a resort (Daniel Daou Ornelas
            Nervion River near Bilbao, with   and Matt Bindner, 2009)
            remediation/cleaning facilities and

and Emerald Necklace (Boston), the Hoover Dam, just to name a few—display an integrated design of transportation and water-related infrastructures. In these examples, a curator bundled various infrastructures in an integrated project—transportation elements, water systems, landscape, and energy sourcing work together. The continuing appeal of these historical projects is the best testimony to the efficacy of bundling. Citizens flow through and interact continuously, experiencing a similar landscape or monument, which itself serves other systemic purposes, bundles functionalities, and creates an awareness or consciousness of place, others, and externalities. The commons begins to operate as a semantic and experiential engine, drawing people into itself. Reduced to its most abstract quality, we could argue that the common quality established by bundling is one of continuity in experience between the space inside the transportation infrastructure and the space outside of it. As a result, one's cultural experience in mobility is not that of isolation but, to the contrary, of participation. Moving about becomes a means to understand the city around us as well as a means to establish moments of legibility and the understanding of society and one's place in it.

Bundling, multimodalizing, and multitasking have not happened in the United States for a while. This is because the postwar welfare state, in its urge to produce functional necessities, completely sectorialized the production of space between different agencies—each with its own funds, protocols, and priorities over different levels of government. Fragmented lines of production have effectively sliced the commons into a series of discrete pieces, disconnected from their very inception. Who will produce these commons, these monuments? The Department of Transportation? The Army Corps of Engineers? The Environmental Protection Agency? Development authorities? Or, as increasingly happens, private development companies?

New commons can be built by "coalitions of the willing." These involve various agencies working together with community groups and private groups. Replacing urban planning's exhausted dichotomy between top-down planning and bottom-up participation, the coalition of the willing signals a new model. The Federal Department of Housing and Urban Development, advised by Henk Ovink, is testing and developing this model in a suite of post–Hurricane Sandy recovery projects in the New York–New Jersey–Connecticut area. Ovink's contribution to the conference explains that by making federal funding dependent on the success of the coalition-building effort, single-functionality thinking is suddenly halted. Bundling designs helps generate a coalition of formerly dispersed agencies. Thus, a new production model becomes possible. In the conference, historian Jo Guldi also addressed the potential of crowdfunding for the production of (smaller) infrastructure projects. Crowdfunding and alliance-building are not theories; they are being tested and developed and can become important alternative means to produce infrastructural commons.

Finally, the title of this book is not "The Commons," but *Infrastructural Monument*. The urbanism debate in North America has been polarized since the 1950s about the rise of suburbs. The latest iteration is articulated in terms of "landscape urbanism" or "ecological urbanism," versus highly urban "compact city" (density, development) radicals. This book accepts (and shares) the dissatisfaction with our existing (sub) urban order. However, rather than locating the solution in an unrealistic massive drive for reurbanization, let alone in endorsing the continued cresting of every new exurban subdivision, it suggests a project of "dispersed centralization." An integrated conception of transportation infrastructure as the provider of a new commons offers a way toward accepting our suburban reality with a real project to reconfigure its dynamics and engage in a gradual, selective densification of specific areas around a commons. Remarkably, cities such as Los Angeles, with its Los Angeles County General Plan 2035, have already begun to develop policies of dispersed centralization. Hon. James Oberstar, former chairman of the Congressional Committee on Transportation, takes on this challenge in his text.

Infrastructural junctions and commons allow for partial urbanization—introducing fragments and zones of varying suburban and urban density around a rethought infrastructure network, designed as a cultural project that includes intersections, intermodal stations, segments of lines that are multitasking and multifunctional in traffic modes and uses. Such objects we could perhaps call "infrastructural monuments." They would be a new commons for metropolitan regions in North America.

Compiling the many different voices speaking at the conference, the contours of this project for the American city become clear: (1) upgrade existing systems, (2) invest in their multimodal intersections, (3) treat these as moments of collective expression and culture by (4) assembling alliances and crowds to fund them.

Fig. 4   Model of a floodable landscape with hillscape settlement (Matti Wirth and Sagarika Suri, 2009)

1   Upgrade existing infrastructures and transportation lines where necessary. Upgrading means letting infrastructures multitask where possible, letting them be intelligent where appropriate, and bringing them up to date when obsolescence is present. Essentially, use what exists and make it intelligent.

2   Operationalize the intersections between existing infrastructural systems and turn these into multimodal opportunities for density and publicness in otherwise suburban environments.

3   Encourage modes of production based on building coalitions of the willing, using crowdsourcing and other modes of post–welfare state production of transportation infrastructure.

4   Understand that in a civilization based on entrepreneurship and civil society, without a strong role for government, there are very few spaces that are publicly accessible, effectively shared, and commonly used not just by a specific constituency but by all of us. Transportation infrastructure is one such space.

This book demonstrates how different authors and experts, from different angles and fields of expertise, are articulating the above points as a common ground. The conference panels were composed of designers, private-development experts, scholars, and public-policy experts. It aimed to find the contours of coalitions of the willing for a new commons.

In a culturally fractured country, where communities are increasingly formed based on shared viewpoints, income levels, and belief systems, any meeting with others outside of our chosen circles becomes a reminder of the larger fabric of our democracy. Recognizing and developing our transportation infrastructure as a commons—our infrastructural monument—would establish a consciousness of this larger fabric on a daily basis.

the infrastructural
monument

This chapter discusses the unavoidable roles
of transportation infrastructures in relation to
other functions, such as public spaces, markets,
and water protection and management. The
projects discussed in this section exemplify the
critical role of transportation infrastructure as a
fundamentally cultural project, across ideolo-
gies, regimes, and perspectives. Although there
is no formal degree in infrastructure design, its
curriculum would contain elements from history, culture, design, architecture, engineering, politics, and planning. In a society without common religion or ethnicity, the
cultural project of designing singular objects valid for all should be a priority.

christopher lee

henk ovink

pierre
bélanger

james
oberstar

Notes on Infrastructural Monuments

Christopher Lee
Associate professor in practice of
urban design, Harvard University,
Graduate School of Design;
Principal, Serie Architects

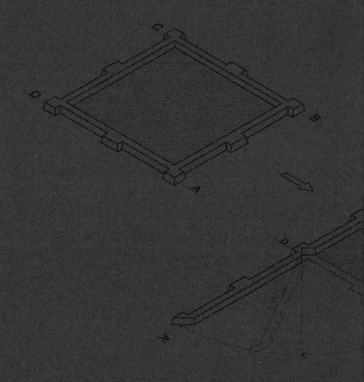

Fig. 2

From a closed quadrangle wall
to an open linear wall, Xi'an
Horticultural Park, China
(Serie Architects, 2009)

I

The assertion that infrastructures are landmarks in the urban landscape is hardly contentious, but to claim that they are monuments requires further qualification. Their colossal size does not alone qualify them as monuments. Artifacts become monuments through their cultural, social, and political significance rather than simply their sheer size. Their significance must be common, for cultural, societal, or political discourses are collective in nature. Thus, I contend that the conception of an infrastructural monument must begin from the idea of the city. This is obvious when we understand that the city, in its idea and structure, defines and reifies our space of coexistence. A monument conceived as such is a common artifact.

II

Architects' confrontation with urbanization challenges through infrastructure design is not a new tendency. In 1976, Reyner Banham, in his book *Megastructure: Urban Futures of the Recent Past*, famously termed the outcome of these efforts "monumental follies."[1] Banham concluded that, like their modernist predecessors, when confronted with the problem of the rapidly expanding city, the architects of the megastructure found that they needed to respond in an equally ambitious and heroic way. Infrastructure, the veins that supply the expanded territory with urban settlement, became the object for design; architecture took on the scale of infrastructure and became megastructure. The designs comprised two parts—a main structure and plug-ins. The first part would be a permanent and expandable structure designed by the architect; the second part would be composed of smaller temporary modules, designed by others, and plugged in to the main structure. Kenzo Tange's Tokyo Bay project of 1960, the movement's masterpiece, encapsulated these principles lucidly and succinctly. Conceived of as an extendible linear city spanning Tokyo Bay, the main spine consists of freeway loops, some inland, some straddling the bay, and some completely in the water. Contained within the spine are civic buildings and places for work and commerce. Perpendicular to this spine are housing blocks, made up of an A-frame, into which dwelling modules are inserted. All parts were envisioned to have their own rates of growth and thus act autonomously but in cohesion with the other parts. Banham's critique of the megastructure is worth noting today. For him, the megastructure is a self-defeating project: by definition, it has to be big to save the world, but this makes it

too big to build. It mistakes pure technical feasibility for political and fiscal possibility. It rehearses the technoscientific positivism of early modernism but on a colossal scale. In other words, the architects of the megastructure took the scale of the solution as the magnitude of its efficacy; they constructed an image of efficiency and functionality

Fig. 3   Model of wall/bridge showing a public square in the foreground, surrounded by amenities and a pagoda-viewing tower designed by others, Xi'an Horticultural Park, China (Serie Architects, 2009)

out of infrastructural aesthetics rather than producing effective or workable solutions. Architecture, yet again, ended up imitating the image of the machine.

III

As an alternative to these technoscientific monuments that are nonfunctional emblems to functionality—resurrected today through digital biomimesis—the infrastructural monument can be conceived of as a common artifact. Thinking about it in this way, we can become reacquainted with the most fundamental definition of the city; as an idea and structure of coexistence. The historical European city can be understood through its dominant types as both rule and exception—housing being the rule, monuments, the exception. This separation between the space of "economy" (housing) and the space of "politics" (monuments, i.e. public spaces or buildings)—that is, the separation between the private and public realm—is embodied in the very definition of the city first provided by Aristotle in *Politics*.[2] The word *polis*, which means "city/ state" and is also the root word for "politics" in English, is defined by Aristotle as a space of coexistence for the common good, that can only come into existence through the act of consensus. Thus, what is common, the polis, is separate from the space that concerns the economic management of the household. Therefore, the city as a common artifact—a monument—is one that stands apart from the extended fabric of housing and the space of urbanization. It is finite, punctuated, and legible.

If at the root of the European city is the idea of coexistence through free will, the root of the Chinese city can be seen as a code of conduct for coexistence. The formation and preservation of a harmonious collective culture has been a constant feature of Chinese civilization, informed by three principal cultural/philosophical concepts: Confucianism, Daoism, and Yin-Yang. These concepts pervade every aspect of life, from statecraft, personal relationships, morals, and ethics to aesthetic production.[3] The conception of the Chinese city is inseparable from the Chinese imperial city from the period of the Zhou Dynasty (c. 1046–256 BCE) onward. The Chinese imperial city was conceived as a whole, its limits predetermined conceptually and demarcated physically by city walls.[4] Here, I would argue that there is no rule or exception. A single dominant type defines the entire city. The quadrangle house, defined by walls and freestanding pavilions, houses all functions of the city, from family dwellings to clinics, temples, schools, and the imperial palace. As a single irreducible structure, the wall gives definition to the various scales of the city and is transparent to program and function. This owes to the way in which the Chinese conceive of the universe as a complete whole—"all under one heaven." The city is thus seen as a large all-encompassing framework. The common artifact here is the wall itself, not as an exception but as a rule.

Through these two ideas of the city, the monument or common artifact is conceived of as a standalone object in one and as a framework in the other. Both examples derive first from the way in which the space of coexistence—that is, the idea of the city—is conceived, which is tied to a cultural and political discourse.[5]

IV

Our proposal for the Xi'an Horticultural Expo is one attempt to draw upon the proposition of coexistence outlined above. The site for this project is located at the northeast corner of the city of Xi'an in China. The project brief was simply to design five greenhouses scattered around a proposed horticultural park that will anchor the expansion of the city at its northeastern corner. We felt this was inadequate in light of the vastness of the urban sprawl of the city; at the same time, we were struck by the beauty and audacity of the tradition of city making in Xi'an. The city wall of Xi'an,

measuring 8.45 miles (13.6 km) in length, is lodged firmly at the heart of the city and continues to form an important anchoring point for the expanding metropolis, despite breaches by the sea of urbanization. As the wall resides in the collective experience and memory of the city, our proposal is an attempt to recuperate this tradition of city making by revalidating the design of the city wall.

Fig. 4   One-kilometer-long multilevel foot-bridge cutting across the park and   motorway, Xi'an Horticultural Park, China (Serie Architects, 2009)

Fig. 5   Interior of wall containing the greenhouses of five climatic zones, Serie Architects, Xi'an Horticultural   Park, China (Serie Architects, 2009)

Instead of a city wall enclosing a quadrangle, we imagine an open linear wall punctuated by walled gardens and supporting public amenities. The wall is reimagined as a one-kilometer-long multilevel footbridge that cuts across the park and motorway, organizing the main circulatory path of the park and its surrounding context. Within the wall itself, the greenhouses are arranged as five sequential climate zones that one can travel through. On the ground plane, pedestrian paths are woven from one side of the wall to another, thereby allowing the encounter of various gardens on the ground as one passes through walls. More importantly, the reinterpretation of the city wall forms a counterpoint to the city center, drawing a historical and cultural link to the city's collective imagination and punctuating a sea of urbanization: a finite framework as a common artifact.

V

To summarize, the infrastructural monument—as an architecture that reifies the idea of the space of coexistence, the collective—can be conceived through the idea of the city. It is not defined by its size, but rather by its ability to accommodate the plurality of the city. This accommodation should not simply result in mixed-use developments—often favored by developers. Despite its varied programming, the main concern of mixed-use developments is the commoditization of time that one spends and the spaces that one passes through in the city. To conceptualize and articulate what could constitute this discursive idea of plurality and its corresponding spaces, we can begin by imagining how to envision a place of respite from these spaces of profit in contemporary urbanism. The infrastructural monument can draw its architectural grammar from the irreducible structure of the city, the very structure that persists and is sanctioned by time and use; for any large structures that disrupt the grain, scale, tempo, and memory of the city will often be rejected by its citizens. This is not a conservative call for contextual continuity or a recreation of an image of the past. It is a simple acknowledgement that there are lessons inherent in the design solutions that have been refined by the passage of time, where each generation revalidates and reinvents these persistent structures, rooted in the cultural history of the city. Even if a clean break from the past is called for, it inevitably begins with the rejection of what precedes it. The infrastructural monument should be a legible and finite artifact, for the possibility to imagine and construct a project of the city today lies not in the design of the totality of the urban environment, but in the design of an architecture as a common artifact that crystallizes the collective nature of our coexistence.

1   Reyner Banham, *Megastructure: Urban Futures of the Recent Past* (New York: Harper & Row, 1976).

2   Aristotle makes the distinction between technè politikè and technè oikonomikè: the former being the faculty of decision making in the public interest and thus politics, residing in the sphere of the polis, and the latter concerning the administration of private space, the house or oikos—the Greek word that is the root of the word oikonomeia, or economy in English. See, Aristotle, Politics, trans. Ernest Barker (Oxford: Oxford University Press, 2005).

3   The closest Chinese counterpart to Aristotle, XúnzÞ (Wade-Giles: Hsün Tzu, c. 312–230 BCE), accounts for the origins of society and the state: "If men are to live, they cannot get along without a social organization. If they form a social organization, but have no social distinction, they will quarrel; if they quarrel, there will be disorder; if there is disorder, they will disintegrate; disintegrating, they will become weak; and being weak, they will be unable to dominate other creatures. Hence they will no longer have palaces and homes for habitation. All of which means that people cannot abandon the rules of proper conduct (liÞ) or standards of justice (liÞ)...there is no way of human living which does not have its distinction (bianÞ); no distinctions are greater than those of social distinctions (fenÞ); no social distinctions are greater than the rules of proper conduct (liÞ); there are no rules of proper conduct greater than the Sage-kings." See, XúnzÞ, 32 Chapters, c. 298–238 BCE; and H. H. Dubs, *The Works of Hsün Tzu* (London: Probsthain, 1928), ch. 5. See also, Fung Yu-lan, *A History of Chinese Philosophy: The Period of the Philosophers (From the Beginnings to Circa 100 B.C.)*, trans. Derk Bodde (Princeton, NJ: Princeton University Press, 1952), 279–97.

4   Nancy Shatzman Steinhardt, *Chinese Imperial City Planning* (Honolulu: University of Hawaii Press, 1990), 12–36.

5   For a more detailed account, see Christopher C. M. Lee, *Common Frameworks: Rethinking the Developmental City in China*, pt. 1, Xiamen: The Megaplot (Cambridge, MA: Harvard Graduate School of Design, 2013), 8–26.

Remarks on a New Era
of Infrastructure Investment

Hon. James L. Oberstar
Member of Congress, Eighth District,
Minnesota 1975–2011; Chairman,
House Committee on Transportation
and Infrastructure 2007–2011

Fig. 6

Hon. James L. Oberstar
(Judith Daniels, 2013)

Lewis Mumford, America's urban philosopher, wrote of the city: "[It] is the form and symbol of an integrated social relationship; it is the seat of the temple, the market, the hall of justice, the academy of learning. Here is where human experience is transformed into visible signs, symbols, patterns of conduct, systems of order. Here is where the issues of civilization are focused."[1]

The World Urban Forum gathered in Naples, Italy, in October 2012 to discuss the theme "Mobility, Energy, Environment." The 8,000 public officials, urbanists, and academics discussed the challenges facing the cities of the future, among which: where to house and how to service the estimated 6.3 billion people who will swarm the world's urban centers in the next thirty-five years—up from the 3.6 billion today. Will cities, they asked, plan for roads, transit, passenger rail, water, and sewer. Will they act to prevent rampant land speculation? Without wise planning, cities will degenerate into slums, miles long. The urbanists proposed auto-free boulevards, rail and bus rapid transit, walkable cities—public transit as the keystone to urban expansion.

It must be our quest, on this threshold of the twenty-first century, to make urban centers of the United States and of the world more mobile, more energy efficient, and more environmentally friendly to support the quality of life that people expect and deserve. In that pursuit, I congratulate MIT for launching the Center for Advanced Urbanism and for convening forums such as this, which will bring to bear the best minds and most thoughtful ideas on the urban challenges of the present and the future.

From 1895 to the end of World War II it was possible to ride a streetcar from New York City to Chicago—with one exception, around Toledo. It was possible to ride a high-speed train from the Twin Cities to Chicago on the Milwaukee 400—400 miles in 400 minutes. The "fastest steam locomotive in the world," said the cover of *Time* magazine in 1935. "Why, it can travel at 100 miles an hour." But then came the end of the war and an explosion of pent-up consumerism and a love affair with the automobile. Streetcar tracks were ripped up, roads built in their place; people soon fled the congestion-choked city to suburbia in search of mobility and personal freedom. The automobile devoured—"*stole*"—our public space, our "commons." Then came the solution: the Interstate Highway System, a transportation revolution to save Americans from a path toward 100,000 highway deaths a year and the congestion besieging the urban landscape.

G. K. Chesterton wryly observed that "a revolution is a continuous turn in the same direction until it brings you back to where you started." That is exactly where we find the state of transportation today: stuck in traffic, wasting $120 billion a year, degrading our quality of life, and diminishing productivity at the very time that population movement is bringing people back to the city in search of community. Figures from the last census show that 75 percent of the population growth has occurred on 3 percent of the land. Urban centers have 15 percent of the highway mileage of the nation, but 50 percent of the vehicle miles traveled, yet cities produce 80 percent of the nation's GDP. The city—Mumford's crossroads of civilization (as I paraphrase him)—needs an update.

To the rescue has come a transit revival—light rail, commuter rail, streetcars (the hundred-year-old success story, rediscovered), circulator systems, bus rapid transit—and with it, reenergized cities and intercity high-speed rail. During the last several years, transit has added one million new riders a day, for a total of 10.5 billion transit trips last year—sparing urban dwellers millions of pounds of carbon, nitrogen oxide (NOx), and sulfur dioxide (SO$_2$) and reducing our dependence on Middle Eastern oil. If we increase transit use to a 10 percent ride share, we could reduce oil imports by five hundred million barrels per year and cut consumption by 40 percent.

And another old-new reality: that transportation, mobility, economic growth, housing, land-use planning, and environmental sensitivity must be done together, concurrently—not in silos, not in isolation from each other, but as a collaborative venture of urban planners and traffic engineers. Jan Gehl, architect and urban design professor emeritus at the Danish Royal Academy of Fine Arts, wrote, "Cultures and climates differ all over the world, but people are the same. They will gather in public if you give them a good place to do it." "People are drawn to public places, where they find other people. We all need those places—good public places," says Neal Pierce.

Gehl describes the opening of Copenhagen's central pedestrian district in 1962—with protests by urban shopkeepers, who said that it would "kill their businesses." Now, everybody is happy with it, and "some even claim that it was their idea," says Gehl. Kathleen Madden, of the Project for Public Spaces in New York, writes, "The street, the square, the park, the market, the playground, are the river of life." These are places where people meet, talk, sit, relax, read, and feel part of the broader whole, says Pierce. The urban design of the future must be one that recaptures the "commons," the "village green," and preserves public space for the people. Real estate—residential, commercial, and business—served by public transportation can command higher rent and maintain higher value than similar properties not well served by transit. One of the most stunning examples of the economic development benefits of transit is the Dallas Area Rapid Transit (DART).

Case Study: DART

The city of Dallas and fourteen surrounding cities established the DART in 1983 with a 1 percent sales tax as the funding mechanism. Years of contentious resistance and support from adversaries and proponents gave way to construction of the Red Line in 1996 (completed in 2002), followed by the Blue, Green, and Orange Lines—eighty-six miles (138.4 km) in all—and the Trinity Railway Express (TRE), linking the city centers of Dallas and Fort Worth. DART logged 252,900 weekly riders in 2012, and over five billion dollars in private sector venture capital investment was generated, attributed to the presence of the DART rail station.

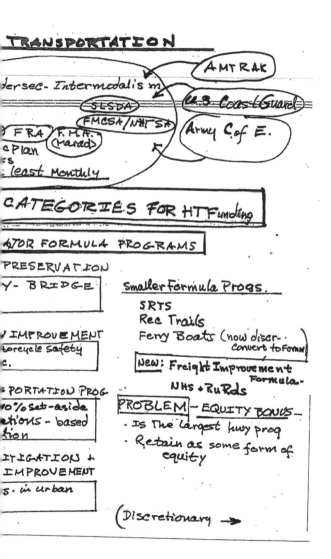

Case Study: The Hiawatha Line

This Minneapolis light-rail success story began as a multi-lane urban freeway proposed in the 1980s. When it was vigorously opposed by residents in the designated right-of-way, the Minnesota Department of Transportation abandoned the freeway to design a light rail in the same corridor. The 11.6-mile (18.6 km) Hiawatha Line (since

Fig. 7   The future of U.S. transportation
(Hon. James L. Oberstar, 2009)

named the Blue and Green Lines) entered service in June 2004, serving the city center, the Metrodome, Target Field, the Minneapolis/St. Paul Airport, and the Mall of America. The line carries thirty-one thousand riders daily and logged 10.5 million riders in 2012. It will soon be linked to St. Paul's Central Corridor Light Rail, serving the State Capitol complex, St. Paul's historic Union Depot, and its Amtrak station.

People who live along Minneapolis's light rail apply for jobs in the line's vicinity; companies retain employees and attract new ones because the line is a magnet, drawing people and economic growth to the corridor. For example, Mark Fabel of McGough Development, the master planner for Bloomington Central Station, a mixed-use project in the Twin Cities, is now developing a fifty-acre (20.23 hectare) mixed-use site in the corridor that includes four hundred apartments and a market rate three-hundred-room hotel. It is a billion-dollar venture when fully developed, with a rail station at the center and a two-acre public park. McGough cleared 500,000 square feet (46,452 sq. m) of former control-data-company facilities to build this project, which is sold out, because new residents will be close to transit.

As the transit revival breathes new life into America's urban centers, the "infrastructural monuments" of the nineteenth century—those single-use railroad terminals and depots—instead of designating the end point of a trip, are being converted into launch points for travel and templates for a lifestyle of the future. These infrastructural monuments of our transportation past have become intermodal centers, exchange points that liberate the human spirit; they are revitalizing Mumford's crossroads of civilization to become our cities of the future.

1   Lewis Mumford, *The Culture of Cities*
     (London: Secker & Warburg, 1940), 3.

The Alliance, Design, and Politics
of Infrastructure

Henk Ovink
Principal of Rebuild by Design (RBD)
and senior advisor for Secretary Shaun
Donovan of the US Department
of Housing and Urban Development
and the Hurricane Sandy Rebuilding
Task Force

The economic, cultural, social, and ecological issues we are facing are increasingly also spatial issues. The confrontation of these issues has a maximum spatial impact on our cities and urban regions. At the same time, there is a growing disconnect between design and politics. This double crunch asks for an urgent reconfiguration of planning and design strategies. There is no one silver-bullet solution that by implementation can change and deliver prosperity or resilience. Applying one solution denies the complexity of our world and the issues at stake. If we simplify reality, it will quickly catch up to us and make our efforts to reduce it to one answer utterly meaningless. Embracing complexity might be the single process that builds approaches that are meaningful in every way possible.

And this is exactly what distinguishes Rebuild by Design (RBD) from other innovation initiatives. RBD started from the premise that to define innovative solutions and a new standard for resilience requires working together as politicians, designers, scientists, engineers, sociologists, and citizens to understand complexity. Through a collaborative process of research by the best of minds in cross-sectoral teams, the initiative touches ground everywhere in the Hurricane Sandy–affected region and interacting with all stakeholders on all levels, scales, and issues. This process provided a suite of opportunities for rethinking resentment on another level, with a real goal toward implementation. RBD embraces the complexity of governance, politics, and the issues at stake to come up with ambitious proposals that will change the world.

Design ensures the confrontation of all types of issues, such as the organization of actors and analysis as well as the identification of both a process forward and on-the-ground interventions that together build a comprehensive approach. Sharpness in confrontation is necessary in order to make choices; this focus will catalyze development and dynamics. Design makes tactile what is only envisioned in policy papers or thoughts. This design approach confronts specific challenges in the different and specific places. Additionally, it sets off the alliance of these main actors: governments, developers, industry, designers, and scientists working together on urgent planning, innovation, and development tasks.

Within this complexity spatial planning can no longer be a trade-off of interests, nor should it result in the allocation of program. Instead, spatial planning moves within the boundaries of leading and supporting, between giving direction with a clear narrative in policies, in laws and regulations, and through programs and projects, all contributing to the wider perspective of social, economic, and cultural tasks. Planning should facilitate, even follow, initiatives to make room, or better, "space," for new physical, cultural, and institutional developments. This stretch, this arc of operation, is precisely what makes planning political—a planning that is socioeconomically and culturally driven and connects with society's demands. This is a process of planning that confronts and resolves the different challenges with the power of the places.

This type of planning calls for design excellence to make explicit and confront differences rather than finding generic solutions. The MIT/ZUS/Urbanisten team for RBD showcases the shift from a policy-oriented process-driven approach exemplified by the profession to an activist, political, and clear-cut design process. Planning at

Fig. 8   Rebuild by Design, bird's-eye view   (MIT CAU + ZUS + Urbanisten,
          of the New Meadowlands project,   2014)
          with Manhattan on the east

the political table shifts its trajectory and embraces research by design as a political tool for an activist approach where there are urgencies at stake. In the Meadowlands project, MIT/ZUS/Urbanisten turns around the instrumental, process-driven, and design-oriented political approach for a clean-water factory that reduces risks and stretches the boundaries for development into the ecological domain. This project shows that it is possible to plan politically and ecologically sound environments with a long-term strategy and short-term interventions. MIT/ZUS/Urbanisten shows that design and innovation become leading factors in these development processes, repositioning design and political capacity from the center of the alliance.

This collaboration through alliances is key. Because we elect people to govern us does not mean that we also delegate all responsibilities to them. They cannot have all the necessary expertise, ideas, or financial means to solve problems alone. The debate over top-down and bottom-up planning approaches is also a false dichotomy. It is not because a government does not decide everything at the top, and because committed citizens succeed in launching the transformation from the bottom-up, that national and urban governments are jobless. It means that the role of people in these situations, just like the roles and responsibilities of other actors, is changing drastically. Politicians and governments must participate in these alliances. Politics has the unique and leading role in recognizing and facilitating alliances of actors that have the will and capacity to transform our cities. These alliances entail strong collaborations with a clear focus in order to respond to the urgencies and issues at stake. This broad mix of collective thinking on all levels and scales and a dedicated focus leads to successful developments. Entrepreneurial attitudes among partners, including government organizations, is essential. Alliances start where challenges emerge and facilitate to support direct interests of people, organized and nonorganized. Good government must identify them as highly powerful collaborations. Governments should participate, facilitate, and give these collaborations a stage on which to act.

The alliance is also a sidestep out of our blocked condition of predefined sets of actors, rules, instruments, and politics. This predefining comes from the hopes we develop of a better future that we can pin down in guidelines, so-called certainties, and perspectives that look like idealistic views. It is a search for certainties in the ever-increasing complexity of the world. The changing horizons, the redefinition of a basis on which we build and the fluidity of the development process ask us to let go of certainties but tend to elicit reactions that are more strict, more predefined, more "certain." It is the alliance that creates space of the in-between, the stretch in time and place that connects and at the same time opens up for reflection and collaboration.

The alliance is the sidestep out of our already impossible, or at least too complex, configuration of rules and regulations, inertia in society and bureaucracy, and the impossibility of acting as individual players of governments, developers, investors, designers, researchers, and business. If we want to change the world we have to let the alliances cut right through to the heart of the individual actors and help reform, as agents of change, these individual and collective powers.

Only then is the "change of the world" about an agenda that enables different actors to develop, research, educate, execute, rule, reign, and reflect. This agenda is not a blueprint nor a guideline nor the prediction of how to make the world better. No, the agenda is the process of change. The agenda leads the way to forming alliances, connecting specific places, people, and issues. And the agenda, in itself, should be adaptive, changing with every step of development.

It is this agenda that connects partners to create facts on the ground. The sidestep is necessary to provide room for innovation and experimentation for the necessary new standards. The ability to test and reflect on the process of planning in real time, with all engaged partners, is possibly the only answer forward. It acknowledges the fact that the current governance, policy, and investment conditions are far from effective. The collaboration and the projects that emerge, the tests of a new and better world, do not create a new institutionalized world. No, the reflections upon these processes, the results of the ideas, design, implementations, and innovation in collaboration, pool back to all the partners involved. The alliance and the projects become Trojan horses for real change within the institutional world—rethinking by remaking, restructuring by collaboration, revolution through design. Again, RBD is the sabbatical detour, the sidestep out of the ordinary, and the Trojan horse at once. It embraces every stakeholder in their formal capacity to lift them up and reconnect them with reality through design. The process also allows stakeholders to reform their own contexts and roles of their formal positions. RBD is not about creating designs in a void but rather, in the real world. It brings reform within policy, rules, investments, politics, and collaboration by detouring traditional paths and creating facts on the ground.

This is about the designers. They must shift positions again and again. Doing everything at once for a sharp and strong perspective in process, outcome, and engagement. This change of knowledge and experience starts in our schools, in our universities, schools of architecture, our centers of practice excellence. The educational, practice, and research institutes become partners within these alliances and engage with all other actors involved. Looking at their curriculum, their built-up position within society, schools should enter the field of practice more and more without discarding their research objective nor their scientific and academic character. Academia must test in practice and engage in this testing to form alliances with the public and private partners, who also have to take the same step. Within RBD more universities participate than nonacademic teams, with their faculty, their students, and their research programs.

In RBD, it is about all partners that perform and reflect at the same time. We all have to make explicit not only what's at stake but, moreover, how to tackle, present, reflect, and discuss the interventions we develop over and over again. We must find and form the platforms, not only in our institutions but also in the world outside the institutions, in our projects, our testing zones, and in the in-between.

We must test, perform, and reflect, with old, new, and unexpected partners, with more room for the specific, the changing perspectives of every place, out of an agenda that emerges from the collaborations and with a reflective agenda of change for each of the individual partners in these alliances. Above all, these are alliances that make design political again.

Fig. 9   **Rebuild by Design, Meadowband segment along the Hackensack riverfront offering recreational amenities alongside new residential development opportunities (MIT CAU + ZUS + Urbanisten, 2014)**

The Oceanic Turn:
Infrastructure for Inundation

Pierre Bélanger
Associate professor of landscape
architecture, Harvard University,
Graduate School of Design

Fig. 10

Pierre Bélanger
(Judith Daniels, 2013)

Thank you very much for the invitation to speak here this evening. I take the invitation both as a challenge and an opportunity to take a position. I believe there is a need for the two largest and most important universities in the United States to work together—especially given the fact that neither of us offers a degree program in geography—to address large-scale issues that are beyond disciplines, political boundaries, or economies.

There is a question that has been preoccupying me for a number of years, which has to do with trying to understand whether we can think of urbanization or even cities without infrastructure. From my perspective, to understand urban economies beyond the footprints of cities, it is sometimes useful to follow the flows of resources. I have three examples that I'd like to bring forward as evidence.

Hong Kong: Hong Kong is one of the densest and most vertical cities in the world and is lauded for its compactness and sustainability. However, once you examine the infrastructure, a new image emerges. For example, since the mid-1950s, Hong Kong has developed a three-tiered system of freshwater provision. First, it imports fresh water from Guangdong in China, from a river in the delta there. Second, it relies on its country parks system, which covers over 60 percent of the Hong Kong Special Administrative Region. The country parks, although designated as such, are really reservoirs for freshwater. Third, Hong Kong relies on seawater for 90 percent of all the flush water in its toilets. You literally have the ocean underneath your bum. Hong Kong demonstrates that, in many respects, our vision of compact growth and density is dependent on a vast horizontal infrastructure.

The Persian Gulf: Today, we criticize ourselves for the amount of oil and resources that we import. However, in the Persian Gulf, the scales are inverted, with water being more expensive than oil. In addition, many of the cities developing there, including Dubai, have no centralized wastewater infrastructure. They have to export it for treatment to vast plants. There's a great YouTube video called "The Poop Snake," for those who are interested.

The Gulf Coast: Here in the United States, the Gulf Coast raises questions about how, in the absence of particular types of infrastructure, we survive certain climate events. One method is coastal contraflow, the system by which highways are flipped during hurricane season to enable formalized evacuation throughout the Gulf's seven states. People use the reversed highways to evacuate in thirty-six-, twenty-four-, and eighteen-hour stages leading up to a hurricane event.

Furthermore, 25 percent of Americans will move within sixty miles (100 km) of the shoreline. Another 15 percent of Americans already live in a managed floodplain. We are moving to the ocean, and with climate change, the ocean is moving toward us. However, as shown during Hurricane Sandy, which shut off power to over a million people and caused the evacuation of hundreds of thousands of residents, our present infrastructure is inflexible. Current debates focus on mitigating or averting climate change rather than coming to terms with the risks of living at the ocean's edge. We must recognize that disasters of our making can be our undoing, and the real storm is us. We live in landfall regions and hurricane alleys, where storms blow in nearly every year. We are at a crossroads, unable to pay for large, protective infrastructure in an environment of economic attrition, while facing new surge, sea-level rise, and flooding threats. As tropical becomes the new temperate, Gulf Coast regions can serve as models for how to build more flexible and contingent urban infrastructures.

Today, our wealth is locked up underground, in the infrastructure we have engineered. Over a century ago, we buried streams in pipes, made wetlands dry, centralized and combined storm sewers with sanitary mains, and created public works departments to manage these underground utilities as cities were incorporated. Military engineers became civil engineers, and with knowledge from the British, French, and Dutch, converted coastal areas and swampy shorelines into prime real estate. Estuaries became sites for industry and shipping, rivers and streams for manufacturing, fertile coast plains for agriculture. Draining for profit and health became the goal, as articulated by preeminent sanitary engineer Colonel George Waring.

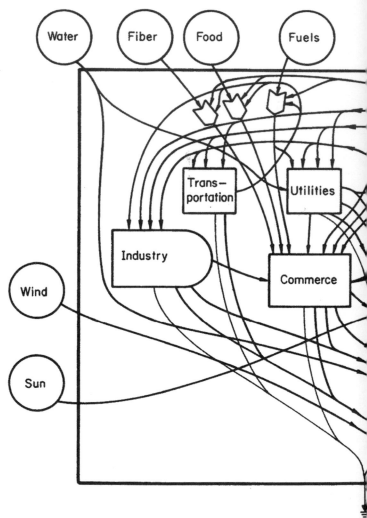

Water was the enemy of twentieth-century urbanization. Growing populations in major industrial metropolises such as New York, Chicago, and Boston faced major sewage and drainage problems. There were cholera outbreaks in the 1890s, and Mississippi floods in the 1920s. The more water systems were ignored, the more important they became as a link between urban economies and regional ecologies. From the 1920s onward, the nation's planners sought to curb the water's influence. From Roosevelt's Flood Control Act of 1944 to Carter's

Floodplain Management Executive Order of 1977, land reclamation became synonymous with flood control. Legislation granted the power to acquire land, build dams, and raise levees to control water levels to the U.S. Army Corps of Engineers, which remains the largest agency of civil engineers in the world today.

To this day, the critical benchmark remains the one-in-one-hundred-year flood level. During the twentieth century, this high-water mark shaped the architecture of structural flood-control measures such as dams, dikes, and ditches. It was also central to the National Flood Insurance Program. The one-in-one-hundred-year flood level is our most invisible national monument, our infrastructural monument. Flood maps, based on this measure, precisely located safe, dry land for development, quantified risk, and established premiums for protection from coastal hazards. We have unquestioningly operated on it for nearly an entire generation. However, (flood) insurance is no longer our assurance. One-hundred-year floods are now occurring several times a decade, or every other year. While the 1993 and 2008 floods in the Midwest may seem exceptional, similar events were recorded as early as 1950. Our high-water mark is outdated and unreliable. Raising dikes or building more dams is not an option. It will put us, if anything, at more risk.

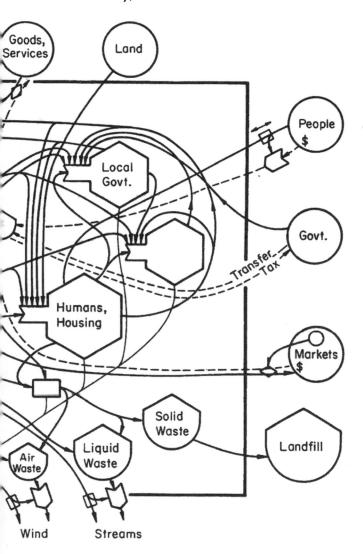

We have to stop looking toward costly megastructures and centralized dam systems that carry significant externalities. For example, the eight thousand locks and dams built by the Corps of Engineers in the upstream Mississippi basin actually starve

Fig. 11   Systems ecology
                           (Howard T. Odum, 1983)

the river of critical sediments, which could otherwise feed barrier islands and shore-line marshes downstream and protect the Louisiana coast. We should look at how other deltaic regions and low-lying coastal areas hold water. In addition, as environmental complexities and uncertainties grow, it becomes increasingly clear that our current land-planning models, water-engineering systems, and climate-change scenarios are, if anything, too precise. They leave very little room for weather extremes, hydrologic adjustments, and ecological flows. In short, we've engineered ourselves into a position with little maneuverability or flexibility. Fortunately, this condition is reversible. The vast ecology of shoreline salt marshes and freshwater wetlands feeding off sediment flow and tidal fluctuations can be redesigned and rebooted.

I want to show a series of photographs as evidence of what we can learn from other parts of the world, where, ironically, there is less civil engineering. Paved asphalt cover can be easily and cheaply modified, underground streams daylighted, downstream pollution averted, and coastal hazards reduced. We can make room for river swells, ocean tides, and storm surges. Property rights are not the issue. Political imagination is what seems to be absent. We can also look to the past. In the late nineteenth century, George Waring and Frederick Law Olmsted collaborated on the design of littoral and coastal lowland landscapes and urban islands, including Central Park in New York and the Buffalo park system. In their work, Waring and Olmsted combined freshwater systems and floodable wetlands with recreational parklands, transportation networks, and institutional services. They designed infrastructure as an urban landscape, with open space for water and room for all classes of citizens. They were the landscape urbanists of their time.

Today, we're facing a new set of circumstances, but we can still work in the same vein by merging urban infrastructure with ecological systems to create infrastructural ecologies. We can not only meet the challenges of river swells, storm surges, and sea-level rise, but also confront other complexities, including sewer effluence, industrial brownfields, and fertilizer runoff at the same time, to achieve spatial and fiscal economy. For example, the transformation of American harbors and shorelines from their twentieth-century Fordist state into new diversified ports and inhabitable waterfronts offers an unprecedented opportunity to reconstruct over the next century. We can build the soft yet structural, flexible yet functional, sensory yet smart infrastructural ecologies that we need now. These landscapes are urbanized estuaries and inhabited coastal plains, downstream from river watersheds and upstream from oceans. They are coupled with underwater sea-grass forests, oyster reefs, and salt marshes to protect the coast and absorb storms. These submerged self-organizing infrastructures promote intelligent forms of inundation, from flood farms to waste wetlands, and are distinct from the traditional centralized infrastructure in the exclusive hands of federal and state authorities. Macroinfrastructure can work with microinfrastructure as well. Small dumb protective mechanisms—generators and water tanks on hospital rooftops, sump pumps in subways, storm shutters, doorway minidams, waterproof basements, waders and boots—can personalize storm preparations and relieve fiscal burdens.

Finally, for the future, we can consider how to lure water into our cities, streets, blocks, and buildings, as opposed to excluding it, as we've been doing for the past century. As sanitation was for the nineteenth century, inundation is our project for the twenty-first. Confronting extremes and indeterminacies, we have to come up with contingency plans that outline how our current infrastructure can work and also fail, where we need to shore it up and retreat.

As we take the oceanic turn, we must also reflect on how to protect ourselves while profiting from flooding, or how to minimize climate impacts while capitalizing on climate change, adaptation, and resilience. Whatever the model of urban change, we, like Olmsted and Waring, search for concurrent benefits: safety and security, ecology and economy, health and wealth.

3
taking advantage of infra-structural redun-dancy

Redundancy is a key design principle for critical infrastructure. Redundancy means that any design needs to include functional and smoothly accessible alternatives in case the main infrastructure becomes, for whatever reason, momentarily dysfunctional. As a consequence, infrastructural fragments or network elements tend to be overdesigned, and generously dimensioned, with backup options. This very principle allows piggybacking various other functionalities and layers of use. Purposefully redundant pieces destined to take over the function of the momentarily dysfunctional main line may in fact perform in many other unique ways during most times when they are not in emergency use. However, redundancy also refers to infrastructural fossils—historical layers no longer in use. Such infrastructures crisscross older cities where they provide invaluable rights-of-way and in doing so offer opportunities to transform the existing grid. The generosity of an older, defunct infrastructure can be of tremendous value. Its open spaces and

don briggs

stephen ramos

robert levit

continuities connect what used to separate, and insert new inventions in the carcasses of the fossils. Redundancy is an almost omnipresent condition in societies with rapid technological innovation and highly engineered infrastructure networks. This chapter discusses the opportunities presented by infrastructural redundancy.

Infrastructural Urbanism

Stan Allen
Professor of architecture,
Princeton University;
Principal, Stan Allen Architect

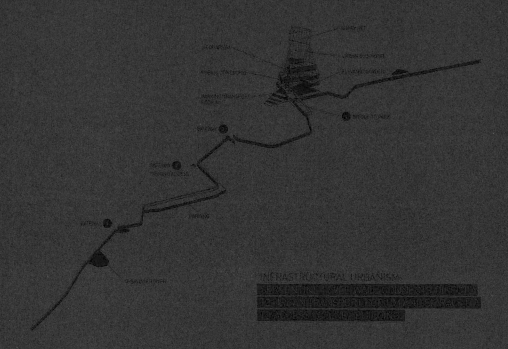

Fig. 2

Yan-Ping Waterfront,
Taipei, Taiwan, 2008
(Stan Allen Architect, 2008)

The real place of the improbable is the city.
— Manfredo Tafuri, *Architecture and Utopia: Design and Capitalist Development*, 1976

Difference is the engine that drives urbanism. The vibrant character of urban life is formed out of competing interests and incompatible elements existing side by side. Cities evolve more than they are designed; the urban field has no fixed boundary and cannot be frozen in time. Everything we value about cities, it could be argued, arises as something in excess of designed intentionality or engineered performance. What cities offer as a political space is precisely freedom from absolute control. If this is the case, how can design, so wedded to control and formal definition, account for the uncertainty, conflict, and excess that are the fundamental characteristics of the city?

The protocols of urban design, as they developed in the 1960s and '70s, kept architecture at arm's length, working through diagrammatic codes and regulations closely aligned with the data-driven language of city agencies and developers. For their most successful adherents, the New Urbanists, architecture is specifically bracketed off from urbanism. The more politically engaged turned to activist urbanism: small-scale, direct actions bypassing capital and control alike but with necessarily limited effect and a lack of architectural ambition. Architects, it seemed, could enter the urban field only by retreating from the exercise of their own disciplinary expertise.

Writing in 1989, Rem Koolhaas suggested a way out of this dilemma: "It requires a second innocence to believe today that urban development can be reasonably controlled...While the built and the solid are now beyond control—subject to political, financial and cultural forces in a perpetual state of flux—the same is not true of the void, perhaps the last subject about which architectural certitudes are still convincing."[1] It is a compelling, categorical statement, and within a decade Koolhaas's remark had been incorporated as a founding insight in the emerging field of landscape urbanism. But to those trained in landscape architecture and ecology, landscape is never empty; it is not a void but a highly charged field, moving matter and energy around, full of life and activity. Landscape urbanism's answer to the problem of city design was to propose, on the model of ecological stewardship, a management regime to steer change over time. Situated at the intersection between regional ecology, infrastructure, open-space design, and architecture, landscape urbanism aspired to be a synthetic discipline that could operate on and within the borders of all these areas of expertise.[2] Landscape urbanism would therefore work not only in the spaces between buildings, roadways, and infrastructure but in the space between disciplines as well.[3]

This was the intellectual and disciplinary context of my 1997 article "Infrastructural Urbanism." Above all, the text proposed a series of working principles by which design expertise could operate effectively in the context of cities and large-scale systems: not by pretending to be able to design and control the vast assembly that is the city but by working strategically, locating key moments in which precisely defined interventions could have a catalytic effect on the life of the city. Infrastructural urbanism, it deserves to be said, was also an aesthetic proposition, based on an attraction to the hard beauty of large-scale engineering design (as opposed to landscape urbanism's celebration of everything soft and green). Underlying the argument was an idea of architecture as a material practice, working in and among the world of things—a conviction that architecture's most powerful agency derives not from its discursive capacity but from its concrete presence as a fact on the ground. But it was also an argument for disciplinary specificity. Instead of moving always down in scale from the general to the specific, infrastructural urbanism allows detailed design of typical elements or repetitive structures, facilitating an architectural approach to urbanism. Any designed structure operating at the scale of the city can be seen as fundamentally architectural: bridges, viaducts, transit nodes, market sheds, levees, and landforms all fall within the disciplinary expertise of architects.

Today I would emphasize the need for strategies that recognize the collective nature of the city and allow for the participation of multiple authors. Infrastructure accomplishes this not by top-down rules or codes but by fixing points of service, access, and structure. Infrastructure creates a directed field to which different architects, actors and agents can contribute. By specifying what needs to be fixed and what is subject to change, infrastructures mediate the precision of design and the indeterminacy of program and use over time. What is required is a new mindset that might see the design of infrastructure not as simply performing to minimum engineering standards but as capable of triggering complex and unpredictable urban effects in excess of its designed capacity.

At the end of the 1990s, in an intense period of experimental design work and writing, I turned my attention to practice, first in collaboration with James Corner/ Field Operations and later as SAA/Stan Allen Architect. Although our work spans a wide range of programs and scales, urban and landscape projects continue to be a major focus of my work in practice. Incorporating lessons learned from the dispersed field of landscape urbanism, this renewed attention to infrastructure represents a reassertion of the specificity of architectural expertise in the design of large-scale systems and structures.

At the Yan-Ping Waterfront we worked to reconfigure a major component of urban infrastructure: the twenty-seven-foot, two-inch-high (8.2 m) floodwall, which presently cuts the city off from the river. In place of a single boundary at the edge of the city, we proposed a system of shaped landforms that open the site to unimpeded access and at the same time create a variety of spaces and programs at the waterfront edge. This strategy maintains the same level of flood protection but increases the number of access points and reinforces the connectivity between park and city. Gently sloped and well-protected surfaces, which can be generously planted, open the city to the waterfront and afford new programmatic possibilities, while the deliberate geometries and hard material surfaces facing the river underscore its condition as a constructed infrastructure. The proposal is a large continuous piece of architecture functioning at the scale of the city.

For the Gwanggyo Pier Lakeside Park we worked with an integrated "field" strategy of landscape restoration alongside a new "pier" structure that bridges land and water. The resulting megaform synthesizes landscape, infrastructure, and architecture. It creates a legible icon that will give the park a new identity, capable of holding its own against the massive development planned on site. The pier itself is densely programmed to activate the site with movement and program. By consolidating all active uses on one strip, the pier serves to protect the remainder of the site for quiet recreation. This landscape-infrastructure strategy not only minimizes the environmental impact and energy use of the park, it returns clean water to the ecosystem, restores the landscape, and generates energy that will enable the park to become self-sufficient over time.

Finally, in our masterplan for Taichung Gateway Park the design work is focused on that which the city government could reasonably expect to control: public open space and roadways. The park and roadway system create a dynamic patch of landscape colonized by plant life, traversed by roads and pathways, populated with people and pavilions, and activated by periodic events and festivals. The "void" of the park is not passive; it is an active living landscape that performs infrastructural work, moving energy and matter around the site and helping to restore its natural and social ecologies.

If the park can be designed and controlled with a reasonably high level of specificity, the surrounding urban fabric can only be loosely steered over time. The city is a dynamic system, possessing its own momentum; the figural void of the park will

Fig. 3   Gwanggyo Pier Lakeside Park,
                 Suwon, South Korea, 2008
                 (Stan Allen Architect, 2008)

appear in time as the city grows. But the park also functions as an attractor, enhancing real estate value and triggering local development. Here our task as architects was to create relatively neutral scaffolding for the city to grow into. We resist the avant-gardism that would insist on reinventing everything within the project boundary and accept the fact that the fabric of the city will be financed, designed, and built by others.

There is a third element, however, that functions to complicate this binary opposition of the void and the full. At the north end of the site we proposed an active infrastructural presence that bridges park and urban fabric. In these large, interconnected, multifunctional buildings, architecture's ability to fix form and structure with high levels of precision comes directly into play. These vast civic and commercial

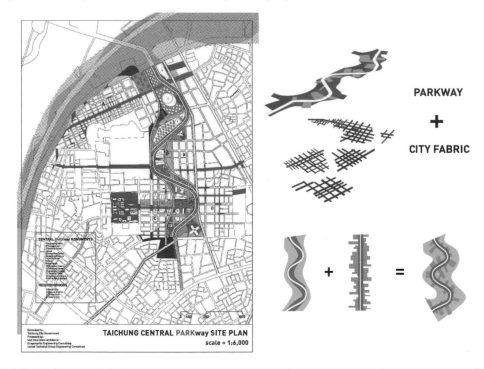

TAICHUNG CENTRAL PARKway SITE PLAN
scale = 1:6,000

PARKWAY

+

CITY FABRIC

buildings (a transit hub, a convention center, and a sports arena) give an immediate identity to the site through the deployment of architecture at the scale of city. They frame and shape public open space, and create infrastructural platforms for a variety of public and private activities.

The city today is too complex for unitary strategies or ideological statements. It requires a pragmatic mix of techniques that parallels the multiplicity of the city itself. Infrastructure plays a key role in each of these projects but it is one among many available strategies. We have learned much from the experiments of landscape urbanism and landscape ecology. The roadways and civic platforms appeal to ideas of infrastructural urbanism, while the strategies for building out the urban fabric over

Fig. 4   Taichung Gateway Park, Taichung,
Taiwan, 2009
(Stan Allen Architect, 2009)

time are not far from the ideas of New Urbanism. To work effectively in the field is to work pragmatically, drawing ideas and techniques from a variety of sources without prejudice or preconception. The architectural strategy we employed in the large buildings, for example, was described by Aldo Rossi nearly fifty years ago. "By architecture of the city," Rossi wrote, "we mean two different things: first the city seen as a gigantic manmade object, a work of engineering and architecture that is large and complex and growing over time; second, certain more limited but still crucial aspects of the city, namely urban artifacts, which like the city itself are characterized by their own history and thus by their own form."[3] This confirms that current strategies of landscape infrastructure belong deeply to the history of architecture's techniques.

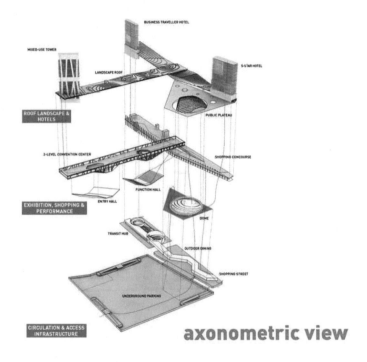

Yet, at the same time these old strategies can be reworked in the present with new design tools, new intellectual templates, and new tasks for architectural expertise.

1   Rem Koolhaas, "Project for a 'Ville Nouvelle,'"
     Quaderns (October–December 1989), 95.

2   Ibid.

3   Aldo Rossi, *The Architecture of the City*, trans.
     Diane Ghirardo and Joan Ockman (Cambridge,
     MA: MIT Press, 1982), 29.

Fig. 5   Taichung Gateway Park, Taichung,
                Taiwan, 2009
                (Stan Allen Architect, 2009)

Maximizing Underused Infrastructure Connections

Don Briggs
President, Boston, and senior vice
president, Development,
Federal Realty
Investment Trust

Fig. 6   Don Briggs (Ana Vargas, 2012)

I'm Don Briggs with Federal Realty Investment Trust. I'm an architecture student turned real estate developer, with a strong penchant for city building. Federal Realty is a real estate investment trust that was established in 1962, and we own a portfolio of retail real estate that is largely community and necessity based. Our real estate is located in primary markets on the East and West Coast, typically in inner-ring suburbs.

About fifteen years ago, we branched out into urban redevelopment and began building mixed-use neighborhoods. We used the fact that because we owned mature real estate we could actually get control of it. Generally, once an owner signs a long-term lease with a tenant, the owner doesn't control the outcome any longer. But with mature real estate, as our anchor-tenant leases become due, we have the opportunity to redevelop the property.

In addition, our properties have typically been located in mature, fully built-out environments near multiple modes of transportation. One project that we started developing in 2002, and completed in 2007, is Rockville Town Square in Maryland. We owned the 1950s vintage strip shopping center facing the other direction, and the City of Rockville owned the parking lot in the foreground. We transformed a suburban context into a very urban context with a human scale.

City building today, particularly when we're talking about transforming suburban context into urban nodes, requires a whole new way of looking at the built environment. In particular, you have to think about infrastructure differently. To us, it's really about identifying existing infrastructure that can support a denser pattern of development, taking advantage of transportation intersections, and introducing a human scale.

In addition, you need to think about the political and financial framework, zoning, and public-private financing tools. It's important to look at a district holistically, ignoring property boundaries. The fractured ownership of property is one of the major impediments to creating a city where one doesn't exist today: not being able to achieve the ideal development pattern because property boundaries get in the way.

I'd like to talk about two case studies today—two of our newest neighborhoods that are under development.

The first is here in Somerville, Massachusetts, about three miles outside of downtown Boston. This project came from five million square feet of entitlements that we had on roughly sixty acres of land on the Mystic River. The first new T stop to be built in Boston in more than twenty-five years will be adjacent to our site. However, when we started, the site looked vastly different.

We bought it back in 2005 and essentially acquired a strip shopping center, an industrial building, the right to purchase some city-owned land, and the right to have the City of Somerville get four parcels through eminent domain. IKEA owned a sixteen-acre (65,000 sq. m) parcel on the waterfront and the state owned roughly one-and-a-half acres (6,000 sq. m) of public

park land that it was using for boat-storage. The site, the Assembly Square District, had been up-zoned dramatically, allowing for much greater density, but was mired in litigation with a community group who, unlike typical NIMBYs, were actually looking for great-er development. However, they didn't want a big box, and IKEA was kind of a sore point. Our idea for the site was to take IKEA's six-teen acres of land and do a land swap with them for twelve acres of land at the back of the site, to recapture the better real estate for mixed-use development. We also wanted to swap the two acres that we owned along the waterfront for the state's one-and-a-half acres, to create a much better park system and extend our development to the tracks.

The plant, as it sits today, has a new T stop under construc-tion. IKEA controlled this site, but they've chosen not to go forward. Our mixed-use development can now extend further, and we have significantly better use along the waterfront. This plan required a significant amount of infrastruc-ture, and we needed to leverage a variety of public and private fi-nancing tools. Infrastructure is not free, and turning an old industrial site into a place at human scale that can also support five mil-lion square feet of development requires a partnership of both private and public capital. The

Fig. 7   **Proposed full build-out of Assembly Row at Assembly Square, Somerville, Massachusetts**   **(Federal Realty Investment Trust, Assembly Row)**

partnership looked something like this: the T stop cost about $50 million, $35 million of which was funded by the state, and $15 million by our firm and IKEA.

The road, which is the spine for the entire district, not the land that we own, was funded through an American Recovery and Reinvestment Act stimulus project. It was a $15 million project constructed by the state. In addition, we cobbled together $65 million of local and state tax increment financing (TIF). Tax increment financing harvests the value of future real estate development and turns it into current capital for infrastructure. Future taxes offer a revenue stream against which the government can issue bonds today to finance infrastructure. We coupled TIF with our own investment to build a finer grain of infrastructure for the development. In a little over a year from now, we'll be delivering a brand-new neighborhood to Boston.

The second case study I want to share is a project under development in Bethesda, Maryland. We own this twenty-four-acre site, which was a 330,000 square foot (31,000 sq. m) suburban power center. We were able to have it rezoned for three-and-a-half million square feet and are currently building a new neighborhood, Pike and Rose.

But the real story isn't about just that parcel. It's about the entire White Flint district. Today, White Flint is 330 acres (1.35 sq. km) of land with typical suburban commercial strip development, but it is located near a metro stop. In 2005, we brought together five other major property owners to form the White Flint Partnership. We convinced the county to up-zone and essentially allow four times as much density as was there previously. Of course, there were significant concerns in a suburban context: traffic, fear, funding. The White Flint Partnership championed solving those problems, building the transportation and financial capacity across multiple properties.

Today, it is suburban, with arterial roads and strip development. Our idea was to create a network of streets, ignoring property boundaries to enhance rights-of-way. Rather than single arterials carrying all traffic, the network spreads transportation demand across the urban fabric. It allows the city to work at a human scale and creates a more walkable community. When we looked at the $500 million of infrastructure needed here, we identified two different pools of beneficiaries. The first was all the county residents, who will benefit from improved transportation infrastructure supporting economic development. We convinced the county to commit some general funds to the infrastructure.

The second pool was all the property owners within these 330 acres (1.35 sq. km), who will benefit from increased transportation capacity and land value. Whether they redevelop or not, their property will be worth more. Believing they should contribute to the cost of this infrastructure, we established a development impact tax for all the property owners within this boundary. They pay 10 percent more in taxes to institute this infrastructure over time. Property owners who intend to redevelop build the infrastructure within their property lines at their own cost.

Of course all of this has to be knitted together, not just in terms of capital commitments but also in terms of phasing. We developed a staging plan with property owners, the county, and the Department of Transportation that enables a certain amount of infrastructure to be built out in conjunction with a certain amount of development. Once that development takes place, it creates revenue to build more infrastructure, which then triggers the next stage of redevelopment. I think this is an example of how we, as developers, residents, and politicians, need to be thinking about our infrastructure environments.

Like Stan [Allen], I was asked about the existence of infrastructure redundancy. However, my answer is not yes; it is maybe. I view infrastructure redundancy differently. For me, the question is not whether there's too much infrastructure, but how we are using it. We spent the last thirty years developing a very low-density environment. We have invested a significant amount of capital, relative to our total amount of development, to service a spread-out building pattern. And I think the opportunity and challenge today, and really over the next twenty or thirty years, is identifying those locations where infrastructure, whether it's transportation or utility, comes together in order to maximize land values and create human-scale environments.

Redundant Infrastructure or
Supply-Based Development Incentive?

Stephen Ramos
Assistant professor, College of
Environment and Design,
University of Georgia

Fig. 8
Stephen Ramos
(Ana Vargas, 2012)

Brian Larkin, in his work on the technopolitics of infrastructure in Nigeria, says the coming of infrastructure is often partial. One town is electrified before another. One hotel has excellent Internet service; another doesn't. This partial arrival of infrastructure effects a split between those who have something and those who don't yet have it.

It produces an experience of temporality, and a desire for the future. It also creates hierarchies in the present, making one place provincial, another central.

This partiality can emerge from a staggered introduction of infrastructure, where one place gets it before another, or from collapse, where one place had infrastructure, and then, for whatever reason, it failed. Sometimes failure can be effectual, resulting in frustration and anger, and fruitful political action. This frustration is always produced relationally. In a way, it is the framework for our discussion today, about how infrastructure is perhaps failing to address the challenges that we face.

Competition among cities and regions to attract global flows involves strategies to offer appropriate infrastructural hardware and capacity, either through better hinterland-market connectivity or more competitive transshipment. I'm going to focus on freight and goods movement. Because of this regional and international competition, development strategies are both proactive and reactive. They involve identifying and capitalizing on internal sectors capable of giving one region a competitive advantage over another but also reacting to moves that other regional members are making to compete for regional business and success. In developing circumstances, as well as in the United States, this can be a gamble. There is a speculative element to supply-side infrastructural provision, grounded in the hope that it will attract the previously mentioned flows. In developmental economics, people celebrate East Asia's success in this regard and lament Latin America's lagging behind in this particular area.

Fig. 9   Atlanta Hartsfield-Jackson   (Hartsfield-Jackson International
International Airport, 2009   Airport)

To think about supply-side capacity, I want to turn to my work in Dubai. In 1966, Dubai was a latecomer to oil exploration and oil discovery. The 1973 oil crisis precipitated hyperinvestment in trade infrastructure throughout the Gulf, with $4.7 billion invested in commercial ports and $3 billion in industrial ports. At that time, the Gulf Cooperation Council (GCC) sought to make collective decisions, agreeing, for example, that Bahrain would be the site of the dry-dock facility. However, Dubai built its own dry-dock facility in the same year, showing the role of infrastructure in regional competition. When the 1983 oil recession occurred, the oversupply of infrastructure led to cost-cutting competition, with clear winners and losers—again, the speculative gamble. Dubai's series of fast projects during the boom period culminated in the Jebel Ali Port Industrial Area and Free Zone, the largest manmade engineered port at the time. It became an induced growth corridor for Dubai's metropolitan morphology, as did other trade infrastructures there.

The Jebel Ali agglomeration, then, became a template from which to structure other trade infrastructural types. The most recent airport, which was hit by the 2008 crisis, but is slowly growing, is clearly structured on the agglomeration and scale of Jebel Ali (e.g. the port as a template for an airport). Moving to the United States to consider supply-side capacity and infrastructure, particularly related to redundancy, we have the current situation where ports east of the Panama Canal are vying to attract trade expected from the Panama Canal widening and deepening. Ports all along the coast are engaged in port dredging and the construction of ancillary infrastructure for circulation to respond to this opportunity. Some interests hope that an oversupply of infrastructure will lead to cost-cutting competition that will make the Panama Canal more attractive to cross and bring some of the trade currently coming through Los Angeles's Long Beach Port to the eastern part of the country. The longshoremen are another actor in this. Their strike in the early 2000s in LA produced a choke in supply that became part of the argument for widening the Panama Canal. The different ports along the East Coast sell themselves according to their proximity to road and rail, their intermodality. This example is about road and rail provisions. So, again, competitive strategies are based on multimodal possibilities: contending for freight on hinterland connectivity.

The US Army Corps of Engineers, about whom we've already heard [in Pierre Bélanger's presentation], is a big player in this process. They're often asked as consultants to study whether a project, a river deepening or port deepening, should be done. However, they are also beneficiaries of the monies that then come for that project. Thus, you have an odd situation where the Corps of Engineers is both analyzing and becoming a potential client for projects, so it's clear that they have an interest in approving them. In addition, the political situation is complex. For example, there is a Savannah Corps of Engineers office, whose purview is essentially the state of Georgia. Because the Savannah Corps office needs Georgia-centric projects to keep it going, it is involved in state politics. Thus, in considering redundancy and competition, I think the Corps is important.

We heard previously, and I think it's a very good point, how the Corps won't do anything that Congress does not ask them to do. That, of course, is true, but at the same time, Congress asks the Corps what they feel is the rational distribution of port facilities on the East Coast. As a result, there's a sort of a back-and-forth between the two, without much clarity, and this kind of infrastructural oversupply is the inevitable result. Of course, one step behind, is pork barrel politics.

If Jebel Ali is a port that informed an airport, in Atlanta, you have a different scenario. In 1960 Atlanta had a very humble airport, the same size as the airport in Birmingham. However, because of Atlanta's overinvestment in Hartsfield-Jackson, it now has the busiest passenger airport in the world. In addition, as officials like to

Fig. 10   **Port of Savannah's Garden City   container facility in North America
                   Terminal. Largest single-terminal   (Georgia Port Authority)**

claim, Atlanta is now five times bigger than Birmingham. Here, again, supply-side investment in infrastructure is tied to regional competition.

In a way, the situation with the Atlanta airport is analogous to the expansions being proposed to the Savannah port. Charleston is less than one hundred miles (161 km) north of Savannah; Savannah and Charleston are currently engaged in port competition, each vying to dredge to fifty feet (15.2 m), so that they can accommodate post-Panamax ships. The proposed channel for the new ships will be thirty-eight miles (61.2 km) long and dredged from forty-two feet (12.8 m) to forty-seven feet (14.3 m) deep. In that sense, it's a tremendous ecological intervention. In a way, it makes one think of Istanbul. It's oddly scenic, kind of an amenity. Even though Savannah has a long river to navigate, it is the fourth-largest container port in the country, which is somewhat counterintuitive. It has the necessary services and distribution centers, related to Alan Berger and Charles Waldheim's work on logistics landscapes in the Savannah area. Garden City is the incorporated area next to the port, where the projected land use changes fairly drastically with the new dredging port project.

We heard a lot yesterday about Hurricane Sandy. To engage in these dramatic port engineering interventions, precisely in the areas that require other types of engineering interventions for climate change, we really are looking down the barrel. There is still a very large need for infrastructural investment that is not clear within the political framework.

So, to finish up with the proposition that we've been asked to consider, infrastructural redundancy, it's a statement in the form of a question, and a fallacy. If you ask U.S. truckers and the people at logistics conferences, they'll tell you there's not enough capacity, right?

And yet, if we're talking about redundancy, the opposite of redundancy, strategy or efficiency, would assume a rational framework. But the political framework is all but rational. Yet we do think of strategy, though, a kind of techno-inevitability of the need for smarter infrastructure starts to emerge. This then gets back to the idea, how are we going to form a political discourse that matches the infrastructural need that the country faces? I don't think we have the political capacity to respond to the challenges that we're talking about right now. If we return to Brian Larkin's work, he refers to the Czech historian Rudolf Mrazek's description of the politics of infrastructure as an enthusiasm of the imagination, referring to the feelings of promise that technology such as infrastructure can stimulate. Roads and railways are not just technical objects; they operate on a level of fantasy and desire. They encode the dreams of individuals and societies and are the vehicles by which those fantasies are transmitted and made emotionally real. My hope for a symposium like this is that we begin to properly articulate these desires, and then the policies and designs that will help us truly face infrastructural challenges.

Infrastructure as Leviathan?

Robert Levit
Director, Urban Design Program
University of Toronto, Faculty of
Architecture, Landscape and Design;
Partner, Khoury Levit Fong

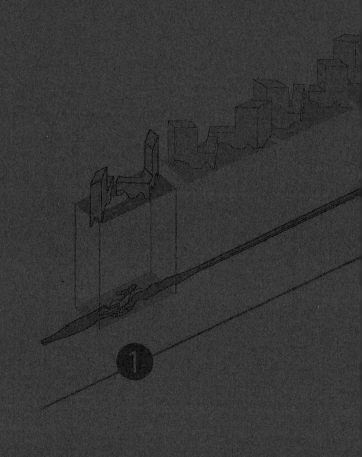

Fig. 11   Nordhavn sustainable city,
diagram of relationship between
proposed subway line, stations,
and towers (Khoury Levit Fong with
Brown + Storey Architects, 2008)

I'm going to talk about two projects that we've done in our office, Khoury Levit Fong. They revolve around the question of how infrastructure lends itself to becoming a site of contemporary collective life and monumentality. I think much of the redundancy of infrastructure relates to how it is deployed in the public domain.

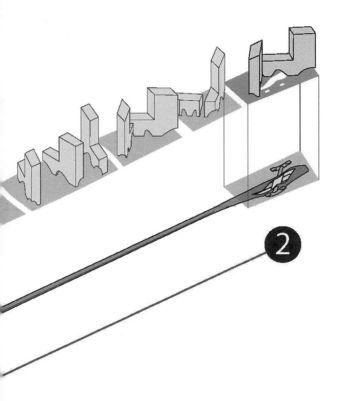

However, I want to start with a premise, which is that it's difficult today for people to identify with forms of collective life, and particularly with monumentality, whether the form of the city or its individual architectural monuments. There is an old program that was used to organize friendships in Facebook, called Nexus. It's now defunct.

I think it's very interesting because it is a social program based on a very atomistic organization: elective affinities. Individuals gather into relationships, of their own volition, but not according to any identification with a top-down, totalizing notion of the social.

We can think of a variety of atomistic organizations of urban morphology and arrangements of dwellings, such as the typical postwar North American suburb. Washington, D.C., is the counterpoint to the idea of a dispersed individuality that makes itself felt in the forms of contemporary urbanism. It stands out in my mind as a very absolute exception, going back to the observation that Washington, D.C., is the uncharacteristic city of North America, New York City is the characteristic one.

I think that looming at the back of the collective imagination is a fearsome image, which is well represented in the famous frontispiece for Thomas Hobbes's *Leviathan*. In this image, individual subjects are subordinated to the king's body. It has become the sort of nightmare specter from which everyone flees today to seek their own individual autonomy. If this is the image in people's minds of what the monument might be, how is it possible to imagine the source for contemporary figurations of collective life? My argument is that infrastructure is the perfect vehicle because its identification with support for life makes it the thing that can garner political support. We can identify with it because it supports what is closest to home: our daily needs. What I would like to show today are two projects in which infrastructure is transformed into monumental figures which give image and form to collective forms of life and daily routines. These two projects are both for cities of one hundred thousand people.

Nordhavn: On the edge of Copenhagen, a landfill site is being transformed into a city of one hundred thousand people. What we've done in this project, a competition entry, is simply take the spine of a new subway extension and turn it into a public boulevard down the center of the site. You can see that there is a series of towers stacked on top of this subway line. When we get into more detail, you'll be able to see how they become a form of monumentality.

I take as counterpoint the famous image of the infrastructural stacking in the construction of boulevards during Haussmann's transformation of Paris. There, you have transportation networks buried several layers underground and buildings above ground with exhaust systems affixed to their facades, which permit air circulation and ventilation down below. However, this combined or redundant infrastructural system is largely positioned as an instrument. It doesn't provide a visible image or turn infrastructure into a form of public figuration.

In our project for Nordhavn, we have attempted to do that very thing: to make the instrument that serves daily needs into a form of collective figuration. The subway runs up the central spine, with this zigzagging pattern of boulevards and a series of tall residential towers stacked on top of it. These towers are combined with the subway station in order to relate the pattern of commuting, and the provision of public infrastructure, directly back to the pattern of dwelling within the city. This is the diagram of the subway coming down the center, with the line running underneath of all these buildings.

This is a typical form of stacked redundancy. Almost all subway lines in dense cities do this very thing, and subways often enter into the public imagination as sites of shared experience. What we tried to do in our project was to emphasize that even more dramatically.

The site is about a mile long, or a kilometer and a half, with two subway stations. These two stations are treated as crevasses that erupt underneath the towers. The towers must navigate the subway's rights-of-way to stand on the available ground for support. When the subway is actually underneath the towers, it opens into a dramatic, articulated set of passages, which let it intermingle with the boulevard space above. Thus, in the ordinary, daily routines of commuting, you are connected more directly to the space of public life, this park/boulevard space which runs above. You can see here the intermingling of the subway infrastructure below and the park space above via this passage to the station.

The other project that I wish to show today is a monumental archipelago, a term that Pier Vittorio Aureli now more or less owns, but I like it too. It's a project for the transformation of a territory about an hour east of Helsinki in Finland, an area called Sibbesborg. It currently has a population of about six thousand people, which is supposed to grow in the next twenty-five to thirty years to one hundred thousand people—an absolutely dramatic increase in size. The site is currently a combination of rural farms, protected natural heritage and ecological sites, and well-to-do suburbs. Thus, there is a question of what form such a dramatic increase in population can take.

Our proposal for the site is a series of islands, which allows us to preserve farmland, hydrological corridors, and natural heritage sites, while intermingling them with

new and existing small-scale suburban housing. The argument I'd like to make about this is that we are preserving and also creating a natural infrastructure here, in the form of hydrological and ecological corridors, that supports the consolidation of new urbanization at the sites. There is a complementarity between the archipelago, or island formation, and the maintenance of the natural ecological system. The consequence, particularly in the form we've established, is that urbanization takes on a monumental figural quality within the landscape, which makes visible this pairing between built form and preserved landscape.

The site of the project has a clear relationship to Helsinki. There is a series of built islands connected by two highways, a commuter train, and eventually, a subway.

Fig. 12   Nordhavn sustainable city, perspec-   towers (Khoury Levit Fong with
                 tive looking toward subway station   Brown + Storey Architects, 2008)
                 and under vaulted boulevard

Fig. 13   Sibbesborg sustainable city,
site plan (Khoury Levit Fong in
partnership with Matar Rahmeh
Studio, 2011)

Within the project, there will be a looped bus service as well as ecological corridors, which were preserved by mandate in the competition brief, and conservation areas, intermingled with the islands of intensification. The hydrological organization of the site produces the island pattern that we have proposed for the project. Alexander [D'Hooghe] brought up one aspect of architectural redundancy in this project, which is repurposing. We have preserved 47 percent of the original roadbeds, repurposing them either for new vehicular service or for bicycle paths and pedestrian paths. Thus, part of the irregularity of the road network you see here is due to the integration of an existing rural road system within the new development pattern. In addition, the site is bound up with the two highway corridors to Helsinki, and with the bus loops, which link to the larger metropolitan or regional infrastructures.

New roadbeds build on the existing cross sections of the site and consolidate them. The islands themselves vary greatly in size and are formally different. Thus,

each of them is able to acquire within the landscape a figural presence, which is similar to the disintegrated or fragmented development patterns of North American suburbs, but in this case, tied together through very tight road networks. We have density studies that suggest how, through different island combinations and variable development patterns, it is possible to achieve the one-hundred-person target of future development. Downtown links to one of the highways and the local road system, and the subway station is underneath one of the bridges.

The boundary figures of the new islands become the visible monumental complement to the preserved open landscape systems. I think the locus of desire with this project is the preservation of landscape forms, rather than explicit, overt forms of the traditional collective image of the city. In other words, it is the preservation of the landscape that is between development. For comparison, I want to reference the famous project by Bruno Taut, the Hufeisensiedlung (Horsehoe Estate) at the south

Fig. 14   Sibbesborg sustainable city, overall   in partnership with Matar Rahmeh
               bird's-eye view (Khoury Levit Fong   Studio, 2011)

edge of Berlin. I see this project as a contrasting project to ours, because the horse-shoe circles a community within the center. It suggests coherence, which I think today is harder to imagine resonating with the social imagination of residents. I believe our project recognizes the conflict between atomized social groupings and the construction of a public domain. I also want to quickly compare our Sibbesborg project to postwar suburban developments. Our project does riff on Radburn, [New Jersey,] which includes open landscapes. The significant difference between Radburn and our project, of course, is the scale at which we are doing it, both at a metropolitan scale and at the scale of the constitutive elements of building.

While Radburn invented an extraordinary new form of landscape for the American suburb, it did so at a very fine, atomized grain that related to the scale of its housing. It became a paradigm for what we call the lollipop pattern of postwar suburbs. In addition, the proposition that Albert Pope describes in regard to [Ludwig] Hilberseimer's idea about North American city development producing fragmented grids of discontinuous elements connected by arterial roads is evident in the example of Chicago.

While our project may bear some resemblance to that North American fragmentation, we think we have proposed something with more highly meshed infrastructural relationships. In addition, by virtue of acquiring a certain scale, it begins to operate in a new urban fashion.

4

marrying infrastructure design and urban development

For most of the postwar period, in the expanding suburban universe of the American city, the production and design of transportation infrastructures occurred in isolation from private developments. Infrastructural grids are produced by the public sector as development generators that are then acted upon by private-sector real estate and design teams. The postwar growth machine was based on independence between the sectors.

Expanding Chinese cities and Gulf cities have followed a similar principle over the last two decades. In all these cases, a strong public sector invests in making large swaths of land accessible, allowing for their (sub)urbanization over time. The

roger sherman

alex klatskin

jo guldi

malcolm smith

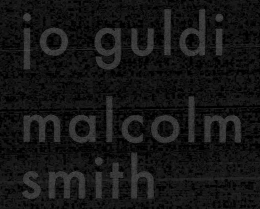

Today, the disadvantages of such an approach are in full view. (Sub)urban realms are internally divided by their transportation corridors into isolated clusters of independent developments. Connections between the latter are rare or nonexistent. Worse, the connections between different scales of transportation lines, which in many cases have attracted some form of centralizing development, are not equipped to handle the latent centrality and potential for public spaces or commons that they inherently possess. This chapter addresses the opportunity to align infrastructure production more closely with urban development.

Battery Power: Recharging Architecture's Causes and Effects

Roger Sherman
Adjunct associate professor and
codirector of cityLAB, UCLA;
Director, Roger Sherman Architecture
and Urban Design

VIEW OF LIRR PLATFORM

Fig. 2   Ronkonkoma Parks and Rides,   (Roger Sherman Architecture and
                                Long Island, New York, train   Urban Design, 2014)
                                arrival/departure hall.

Those who have at any point over the past thirty or so years followed the discourse on the design of the contemporary city cannot help but be led to the conclusion that the architect's last hope by which to shape and discipline an increasingly unruly and uncontrollable metropolitan condition is through its networks of infrastructure. The preponderance of empirical evidence, however, gives precisely the opposite impression: that if anything, infrastructure has in fact been and continues to be the prime culprit at the root of a now century-long marginalization of architecture's role in shaping urban experience. Technocratically conceived and managed, these ubiquitous

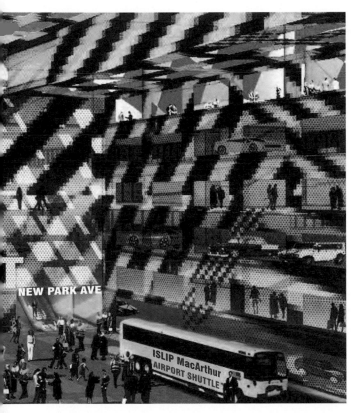

NEW PARK AVE

ISLIP MacArthur
AIRPORT SHUTTLE

public rights-of-way and open spaces are indifferent to the buildings alongside them. Recent sea changes in the politics and economics of cities, though, suggest that a reconfiguration of the manner in which public services are delivered is underway, offering an unprecedented opportunity for architects to challenge the traditional exclusivity of infrastructural design and its primacy upon performance/optimization/maintenance/safety at the expense of a more integral visual and spatial relationship to the building fabric that it supports.

Even as it has never been more dependable and efficient in collecting and distributing resources, waste, and people, infrastructure has progressively become spatially disconnected from the experience of the city it serves. It is difficult to fathom that just a century ago, long before the advent of best management practices (BMPs) and so-called smart cities, the experience of urban space was shaped by buildings. Spaces of movement directly and visibly engaged the private properties that fronted them. Architecture was invested with, and negotiated between, a dual agency corresponding, on the one hand, to the agenda of its sponsors, and on the other, to an instrumental role in the life of the city, in which it served as a prop. Colin Rowe used the term "set piece" as a means of arguing for the public status of (even a private) structure on the basis not of its objecthood (a critique of the modernist legacy) but as a setting or backdrop capable of attracting, supporting, and even inciting unplanned public events and actions.

This model of urban building ended in the early twentieth century with the rise of planning as a discipline distinct from architecture. With more efficient delivery systems for water, power, and transportation, requiring a skillset in management and logistics over that of the orchestration of appearance, the relationship between the two fields became progressively more detached. Today, the "design" of the flows of water, waste, power, vehicles, etc. has grown in primacy to the point that these territories and their concomitant apparatus and performance specifications have come to dominate, de facto, our experience of the city. In so doing, they have interceded in the formerly direct relationship of buildings and the public spaces adjacent to them—distancing and neutralizing the possibility of extending architecture's affects and effects beyond its immediate situation. Not surprisingly, the agency and instrumentality of Rowe's approach has been degraded into mere "background" or "infill" building—as those more passive and demure terms suggest, certainly "not architecture." Yet despite this, the instrumentalization of infrastructure as the primary disciplinary tool of city making has ironically become a standard belief and practice—even a calling card—for many architect/urbanists who seem oblivious to the insufficiency of the former practice, which is pure expenditure, and its (albeit indirect) reliance on the inglorious profit-driven nature of the latter. (The false dichotomy between them seems doubly ironic in this light.) Other architects, meanwhile, have at the opposite extreme taken this same detachment as license to pursue a solipsistic rhetorical agenda more interested in autonomous expression than collective engagement.

Since the Reagan era, however, this now century-old extensive systems model of infrastructure has proven increasingly difficult to implement. Onerous processes of appropriations, approvals, construction bidding, and oversight have made the public sector incapable of delivering projects in as timely and cost effectively a manner as its private counterparts. In response, government overseers have resorted to incremental, piecemeal, or pay-as-you-go methods of execution, resulting in a brand of infrastructure that resembles deferred maintenance rather than heralding the larger-scale public initiatives that characterized its WPA-era heyday. Not simply attributable to the 2008 recession and mounting government deficits, such a development is both a cause and symptom of an increasingly distrustful and self-interested public, and its steadily growing reluctance to fund projects of larger collective benefit. Whereas infrastructure was, at its turn-of-the-century inception, accompanied by a public enthusiasm for and even marveling at the effort behind the delivery of the services it provided, that wonderment is today accorded to the effortless instantaneousness of digital connectivity. Whether in surrender to or ignorance of this fact, planners have adopted a decidedly lowbrow approach to infrastructure's appearance, preferring to keep it as perfunctory and efficient (cost-effective) as possible, lest it become a symbol of government waste.

Silver Lining
The lack of public appetite for capital investment in infrastructure has resulted in the devolution, if not outright failure, in both the quality and scale of the network

model, despite its many adherents in the design and planning communities. This has coincided with a fundamental game-changing shift away from the primacy of infrastructure as an a priori, extensive, and world-building instrument to one that is opportunistic. More localized in its scale and reach, the new "battery-powered" approach is premised on self-sufficiency and is financed and delivered by the private interests whose own properties it serves. In a political environment that is increasingly risk-averse, public officials have moved beyond the mitigation measure in exploring how taxpayer risk can be better managed by delegating to the more disciplined private sector the responsibility of developing, designing, and constructing public facilities in conjunction with the latters' own projects, limiting government involvement to matters of compliance with public policy and technical oversight. Public participation is not eliminated but is instead strategically leveraged—in the form of subsidies, tax breaks, and entitlements—as a carrot aimed at rewarding/incentivizing private development initiatives willing to assume the risk (cost, liability) of building public amenities into their pro forma designs. Rather than being provided as part of a larger connective network, as before, they are piggybacked on and within each project/property, on a circumstantial/individual basis.

The Gambit

Freeing infrastructure to assume a more leveraged approach to providing public amenities absent the fixed-sum metrics of efficiency and optimization, privatization signals a shift from its limited role of service providing to a more entrepreneurial one of destination making. For both developer and architect, it offers the opportunity to enhance their political agency, using programming and design as a double-jointed proposition acting as both bait and hook: first, the fixed-sum dynamic of NIMBYism (and the defensively minded mitigation measure) is eschewed in favor of a calculated strategy of trade-offs, whereby the built-in public benefits it promises are used to sweeten stakeholders' collective pot, as a means of eliciting support. Second, those same surplus amenities are capitalized on to widen the project's catchment/audience beyond the bounds of the property itself. In opposition to conventional infrastructural planning, which increasingly finds itself in a perpetual game of catch-up to simply meet current needs, this new privatized model is directed toward supplying and evoking desire for what is not there (yet). It looks for opportunities, hidden in plain sight, for disruptive innovation. From new forms of (public) parking and recreation to mobility centers, it explores modes and mixes of access and excess, opening private property to (qualified) public use while building in excess capacity for wider community participation/enjoyment. The success of recent such efforts, undertaken without public subsidy or incentives, is proof that leveraging private development (at least in part) as a gizmo by which to seed and stimulate the social desires of their local surrounds yields reciprocal benefits to the project itself.

Just as this newfound legal and financial interdependency between government and private development blurs the line between public and private domains, it also provides a format in which to remarry the disciplines of architecture and planning for the first time in over a century. For the former this translates to an unparalleled, if circumstantial, opportunity to reclaim its agency and instrumentality in city making. The shift away from the network model of infrastructure to one that is battery powered and local relocates the provision and design of collective amenities to the scale and format of the individual building and the orchestration of the way in which it engages adjacent space(s). For design practice itself, profound ramifications lie in the shift from infrastructure as born of necessity to one that arises to elicit desire/wants—that is, invented to attract new markets. Predicated upon a fundamental reconsideration of the public as neither assumed nor uniform, such an approach sees the city rather as comprising a virtually infinite and complex array of distinct yet overlapping subcultures—of which our culture at large is now constituted. As the revolution in

television programming powerfully attests—from a few similar networks to an ever-expanding selection of niche-oriented cable channels—these audiences lie hidden in plain sight, while others are in the making.

In contrast to public infrastructure's logic of optimization (how best can something perform), the battery-powered model is charged by the uncanny possibilities of orchestration: how else things might work. In an era of unprecedented digital connectivity, characterized by a sharing economy that prizes access over ownership, the explosion of new forms of identity discussed above holds an unprecedented potential for the design of new formats of propinquity—formats more unique and exotic than the ubiquitous "work, live, and play" nomenclature that constitutes the sales pitch of much current private development. For the same reason, this means they must also be more plastic than the single-purpose infrastructural products of yore (i.e. parking or recreation or farmer's market, etc.). These more eccentric yet functionally indirect or uncertain arrangements by which to stage collective activity have the effect of disrupting the internally oriented logic and conventions of type, opening them both to externalities and to speculation about new forms of unscripted activity of which urban life might consist today.

Two projects serve as brief illustrations. The first, a series of proposals for Target Corp., explores how the design of its big-box retail outlets might be adapted to urban markets where it faces increasing NIMBYist opposition and land is too high priced to employ surface parking. The architectural strategy-cum-business plan acts as a Trojan horse of sorts: one that proffers a new politics of urban space and collective life, drawing from the social cosmology that appears on Target's own website. Each

project is sited in a geographic context in which there is an undersupply of the particular resources it offers (the props for which may all conveniently be found in the store inside): TargetPlay offers a new type of urban recreation space in Brooklyn, TargetGreen is a repository of all things green in parched Phoenix, and TargetTown provides an ex post facto town center for an exurban development lacking one. All three are staged on a monumentally scaled sloping surface fronting the box itself, under which multilevel parking is tucked. Part billboard, part landscape, part stage, the incline blurs categories of ground and facade, catch basin and catchment. Tattooed with Target's logo as a form of 2-D primitive, it broadcasts to passersby as well as to Google Earth. A more robust public presence, rather than one mitigating local impacts, enables its private sponsor to garner community support in exchange

Fig. 3   Thinking out of the big box,   (Roger Sherman Architecture and
                TargetTown, Tracy, California   Urban Design, 2009)

for offering amenities that government is unable to. It demonstrates the company's commitment to community health while at the same time extending brand recognition through an in situ demonstration of its brand as lifestyle.

The second example, Ronkonkoma Parks and Rides, stands at the center of a town that never was, a rail hub designated at a time when New York City was dispersing into its suburbs. Now that the polarity has reversed, market studies suggest an opportunity to insert a slice of Manhattan's energy, density, and intensity into eastern Long Island—a major summertime destination—where there is also latent demand for family-oriented commercial activities, judging by the large number of affluent family households there. Today, however, the current station is little more than a point through which passengers transfer from auto to rail transport, confined to weekday

morning and evening commutes; minimal time is spent there before boarding and after alighting, with low levels of utilization on weekends and evenings. As a result, the massive 3,550-car commuter lot is either jammed (weekdays) or empty (nights and weekends).

Parks and Rides leverages the single-purpose utilitarian status of the site, as well as its strategic location at the intersection of planes (a regional airport), trains (Long Island Rail Road), and automobiles (an interstate), into a leisure and business destination combining recreation, entertainment, hotel, and meeting venues. In so doing, it uses infrastructure as an alibi to reach beyond its captive commuter audience with offerings and experiences to entice area residents and out-of-town visitors: creating a veritable "leisure gateway" aimed at extending the stay/layover of anyone passing

Fig. 4   Thinking out of the big box,   (Roger Sherman Architecture and
                       TargetTown, Tracy, California   Urban Design, 2009)

through the station site. Capitalizing upon the sheer size of the parcel, these activities, bundled together with 25 percent more parking than the surface lot it replaces, provide the critical mass of additional activity necessary to transform the project's larger surrounds. But instead of mimicking normal infrastructural arrangement, with street and storefronts at ground level, housing above, and parking below, the densely packed structure—half garage, half Manhattan—is composed of alternating wafers of parking and tenants linked by ramps and escalators stitching the checkered uses that flank them on every floor. Into these are carved a pair of singularly orchestrated void spaces: a retail, hotel, and conferencing-oriented Park Avenue "East," and a superscaled "soft" all-season recreational venue, offering activities ranging from a driving range, zip line/trapeze, mini golf, go-kart/bike track, and hockey rink to an amphitheater. Only upon landing or taking off from the airport, or on the blimp ride offered on its rooftop, does the hidden identity of the project reveal itself—the Empire State Building at rest—apropos for Long Island, where a large chunk of New York City goes to relax.

For architecture, the extrinsic demands of excess capacity and exaggerated public access exert a much-needed pull upon the gravitational weight of its own orthodoxy, requiring it to stretch its disciplinary scope to recapture that of the design of urban space. In contrast to the solipsism and passive expressionism of the object building, architecture's agency is recuperated in the combinative design of setting and agitprop—scenographic tools aimed at inviting new audiences and forms of collective participation and interaction, transgressing conventional bounds of public and private. In staging these uncanny experiences—which media experts refer to as "must-see" and which elicit the kinds of posing opportunities that Asian teens call "gawking"—this 2.0 version of Rowe's set piece uses the affect of strangeness (via the alteration of arrangement and appearance) as a device to catalyze a parallel set of intended but underlying social effects over time. In so doing, infrastructure is recast as an agent in the incubation of a new generation of infrastructural spaces that instead of playing a residual role in the life of the city, serves as a strange attractor.

San Francisco's Lombard Street (1922; Carl Henry, developer) continues to attract tourists seeking a "must-see" (and must-drive) experience, yet it represents an entrepreneurial model of "deviant" infrastructure that would be anathema to policymakers today. It is precisely its failure to hew to the optimal and standard that is the source of its enjoyment.

Supply-Chain Architecture
and the Public Trust

Alex Klatskin
General partner,
Forsgate Industrial Partners

Fig. 5

Alex Klatskin
(Judith Daniels, 2013)

So I realize I'm with many architects in this room, and I just want to put something out there during the next ten to fifteen minutes. Shipping containers. They start as shipping containers and will remain so for the next fifteen minutes. This is not affordable housing. This is not the [Venice] Biennale. This is not temporary shelter. These are shipping containers. Please treat them accordingly.

The shipping container, I would say, is part of infrastructure. Most of you know the history of the shipping container. Developed in the 1960s and '70s, it was a great aid in supplying during the Vietnam War. It functioned as part of our military infrastructure and allowed us to get goods and arms to a place with very little infrastructure. All it needed was a chassis, and it could move around in an underdeveloped country. What we didn't know was going to happen was that, twenty years later, the shipping container would be aimed right back at us. It would bring the products and electronics and all of the other things that we get from overseas.

When manufacturing shifted from the United States to Asia, particularly China, we developed a port system to bring in bulk. Cargo was loaded and unloaded by hand. The system was at grade with the water. It was relatively flat, occasionally flooded, and was really a barren landscape. The infrastructure in New York City, which I'm going to talk about, which I develop and am interested in, is not particularly human friendly. It is not walkable. It is not cozy. It is not livable. It is not warm. It is not human scale, nor is it entertaining. It is efficient. It is fast. It is noisy. It is sharp. And it is sometimes objectionable. However, it is an important part of getting goods and products around the globe so that we can live in cozy, walkable, livable, warm, human-scale cities. So how do we place these ports of entry, which is effectively what they have become in this country, close to urban environments in order to accept the goods and products that we need but also not offend the neighbors around them?

The idea of mixed use doesn't apply here, unless the other use is another form of infrastructure. So why are these ports relevant to any discussion of infrastructure? Through culture, we develop a need for goods. For example, we consider the things that someone who is a student here might have: a belt, pants, shoes, sunglasses, hair care-products, a hat. Each one of these things travels through the supply chain. The majority of them come in containerized form and have to be distributed throughout the city and the suburbs. What happens here, as we've developed these consumer products and this insatiable need for them, is that we have to move them around quickly. How are we going to do that? We have components of infrastructure for goods movement. For example, there are the containers. Obviously, there are the smaller boxes in which you package things. However, there are also delivery trucks, warehouses, and the ships on which the containers come.

A shirt factory outside of Shanghai, near Suzhou, makes one in six dress shirts in America. So if there are three billion dress shirts in the United States, five hundred million were made in this factory and sent over to the United States. When this product travels around the globe, it does not encounter environments that are walkable or cozy. I will reuse these words because they're an important part of urban development. Instead, the focus is on efficiency, using capital as quickly as possible, and

cycling to the point of purchase as fast as it can. Obviously, there are some underlying assumptions about quality and choice that come through these things. However, it is critical to see goods in this shadow system of movement, traveling around the globe in fast and occasionally unsavory ways. We are clearly not worried about the human experience in this condition. That is not what is on the agenda with goods movement.

One of the good things about large port areas and the system by which these things travel around the country and globe is, that by reserving these great big pathways for goods in the form of the interstate highway system, we have kept the land in the public trust. I think that when we look at big, ugly, fast-moving infrastructure, we cannot give enough importance to the fact that the public highway network, as unsavory as it may be, has developed a system of continuous rights-of-way around the country. For example, the roadways that go along the Charles River here are public rights-of-way, which we could use at another time when we're no longer using this system. There's an opportunity to piggyback infrastructures, whether containers, boats, or the highway system, to have more than one use. For instance, the highway system, like the container, was developed originally for civil defense. The motive was, How do we get troops across the country quickly if we need them? It wasn't so you could drive to Florida really quickly for your vacation. However, the highway system has enabled interstate commerce, as well as transportation for entertainment and business, in conjunction with some interstate commerce laws. It has been something that we've been able to reuse over and over as time goes on. Container and bulk movements—including petroleum, other liquids, and powders like cement—connect the consumer with the producer and are oriented in an east–west direction because of prevailing winds in the ports, which have remained the same since the ports were developed hundreds, if not thousands, of years ago.

I think the scale of distribution is going to change over the next forty to fifty years. Consider the Arctic cap, which may be disappearing. I will be agnostic about the cause but say that it is. I will say that, as we go into the next fifty years, we will see containers and goods move over the top, and not around the side. In some ways, this will be more green because we have a shorter distance. I think we will see urban development happening in the northern part of the globe, in light of trade routes shifting in that direction and the vast natural resources there. What we can't do is control the supply chain, but we can contain it, and we can make corridors for it to work more efficiently.

I'll talk briefly about the pipeline system. There's a pipeline in the news, about which you've all heard. It's creating more press than it probably should. It doesn't look that dangerous, does it? It looks pretty satisfying to me. However, moving liquids and gases around this country and North America in general will become more and more difficult as we get regulatory pushback. We may do to put these things within already determined rights-of-way, whether the highway system or other rail lines. I really think that these should not be on their own.

I also want to talk about breakaway industry here. The cruise ship is one of the most fascinating inventions, not because you could deliver gastrointestinal problems to thousands of people quickly but because you could completely usurp traditional regulation. Why is every ship located in Panama or George Town, Grand Cayman? In finance, we would immediately think tax reasons. However, in reality, the biggest beneficiary of this is labor laws. You can work people twenty-four hours a day and not give them workman's compensation when they're out in the open sea. You're twelve miles (19.3 km) offshore. You can do whatever you want. I propose that the supply chain will be reinvented in its original corridors, but we will manufacture on our way to the destination. Consider the fish cannery. A fishing boat catches tuna, cleans it, puts it in a can, and packages it by the time it arrives at its destination. It's a fantastic invention. Likewise, consider Blueseed. Some great venture-capitalist guys have decided to park an unused cruise ship twelve miles (19.3 km) off the coast of San Francisco. The premise is that there are a number of start-up companies from around the globe with a lot of capital in San Francisco that wants to invest in them, but their key workers can't get visas for the United States. So the venture capitalist people are renting to these people who have great business models but need capital. The ship is basically an office building. The venture-capitalist people take a piece of the company and plan to shuttle capital back and forth. Again, this is taking advantage of regulatory realities, or what might even be called loopholes, to create new industries.

I truly believe we have to be doing two things at once—nothing can be static—and we all have to do within the supply chain what we can most efficiently. We talk about collaborative work. What could be more collaborative than our friends working together along the way? Finally, I would like to say that, in my business of supply-chain and industrial architecture, you can make great buildings. You just can't tell anyone because they automatically assume that they're not as efficient. However, over the last twenty years, we have been able to develop products that work both functionally and financially.

Crowdsourcing: Who Will Design Tomorrow's Infrastructure?

Jo Guldi
Hans Rothfels Assistant
Professor, Brown
University

Fig. 7

Horse tickets
(Yale Center for British Art)

In 2005 James Howard Kunstler's *The Long Emergency* foregrounded the staggering mismatch between contemporary patterns of suburban development, based around long commutes, the automobile, and fossil fuels, and the prophesies of rising costs of fossil fuels and other materials that would make the bulk of American residences obsolete by 2020. Kunstler's image of a suburban town on a high bluff outside Pittsburgh, where the majority of inhabitants drive an hour to work, is a touching portrait of wasted infrastructure—of real estate, building materials, roads, and sewers invested in suburbs. We have known that suburbs and highway commutes should become extinct as early as the Club of Rome's 1972 Limits to Growth report, and since the 1970s, a great many individuals have heeded the warning, preferring dense high-rises and walking cities to suburbs. What is shocking is how many have not heeded the warning and how much of our collective wealth, in the form of state-built roads and bridges, has been spent connecting suburbs doomed to die, rather than building up high-speed trains and extending subways for the cities of the future. What have we been doing, building such antiquated infrastructure for so long?

We could add to Kunstler's warning the mismatch between the pattern of building in flood plains and beaches since the 1990s and the realities of decaying levees, intensifying storms, and rising sea levels. We have not built with the future in mind, and our investments are heaped on sliding sands, destined to perish in another decade or so, taking with them the savings of the middle classes and a great proportion of our national wealth.

What sorts of people will respond to these crises? We all know who designed the infrastructure of the industrial revolution because the engineers were famous. Thomas

Telford's autobiography, sumptuously illustrated with careful engravings of his many bridges and canals, was greeted in the popular press as a literary triumph. Samuel Smiles's *Lives of the Engineers*, which profiled Telford alongside a cast of other foremen, contractors, and designers, became a classic of grammar-school education in the nineteenth century. Those odes to personality were the popular froth above a new monument in the institutional evolution of humanity, the very moment that gave us the state in its first recognizable form.

The state and the civil engineers it employed were responsible for the Hoover Dam, the Interstate Highway System, the sewers of Paris, the reservoirs of the Hetch Hetchy, and the Big Dig. Together, they formed an institutional matrix of politicians, bureaucrats, and manufacturing lobbies that decided that infrastructure represented the best possible investment in the name of the public. This nexus of human energy, invented in Britain in the eighteenth century, created a world of centralized, state-built roads, bridges, ports, lighthouses, railways, industrial canals, and improved rivers. The infrastructure state employed civil engineers in the École des Ponts et Chaussées, the Ordnance Survey and parish roads system in Britain, the U.S. Army Corps of Engineers, and their colonial equivalents. In the course of the nineteenth century, demands on the engineering profession were broadened both in subject matter and in global reach.

The civil engineers who formed Britain's infrastructure state gained power over state, market, and industrial lobbies as a result of a full-fledged information revolution of their own making. For the task of collecting data, they invented mathematical equations to model the embankments they offered to remove; they commissioned scientific instruments to measure friction and horsepower. They paid the best engravers and cartographers in the land to visualize their equations calculating how much time and distance new infrastructure could save the nation. They took advantage of the information revolution of their day—the cheapening of printing and of paper, and the invention of the open printed form—to create a many-to-many information network, where local government officials in every village in the nation were constantly corresponding with civil bureaucrats in the nation's capital about which roads needed to be improved and how this would be done.

In short, the original infrastructure revolution was an information revolution, not unlike the era of the personal computer and smartphone, the source of many-to-many communications today. In the 1780s, when Highland laird John Sinclair began to imagine how Scotland would be changed forever by a road link to London, he started by collecting information with which to persuade Parliament to pay for the first national road system. Sinclair sent letters to every minister in every town in Scotland asking about the number of unemployed men whose lives might be changed by the coming of roads, inventing in the process of correspondence the first sociological survey. A generation later, Sinclair's favorite engineer, Thomas Telford, set about persuading committees to fund his bridges despite their novelty and susceptibility collapse. He too became a revolutionary of information, devising new metrics and inventing prismatic measurements that form the basis of civil engineering education around the world. Without those social surveys and measurements, we would have kept building block-long streets and short-term bridges, much as we had for centuries before.

The revolution that produced infrastructure was an information revolution about coordinating human beings from parliament all the way down to the parish tax assessor. Its foundation was the ordinary business work of collecting vast accounts and measurements, reorganizing them into strong and compelling arguments, and taking that information around to committee after committee, finding clients, and feeding them with the information necessary to secure a stream of funds. Without a dramatic change in the kinds of information about unemployed persons, potential funds, and distances traveled, without a concomitant increase in the number of accountants, surveyors, cartographers, clerks, and engravers employed, infrastructure would have never come to exist as an industry in the first place.

In the era of the Interstate Highway System, much of the drama of engineering disappeared. In the era after Eisenhower, civil engineers looked forward to nine-to-five jobs that were secure for a lifetime. Working for an unchanging authority, they learned to conform to a set of codes for driver safety and structural integrity set up by generations of engineers before them. Was this an institution equipped to reimagine smart cities or respond to global warming? For generations, civil engineers around the world worked in bureaucracies in which few information revolutions were to be found. Institutions changed little; math changed little. Small adjustments in materials and accounting formed the great changes of the day. For at least half a century the institutions that govern infrastructure have not had to adjust to a shift in information, with the result that when faced by new circumstances, they are paralyzed.

The information revolutions designed by engineers to create more sustainable cities are dinosaurs in the history of institutions. LEED certification, for example, with its exams, conferences, and memberships, is the kind of members' club and static checklist that could have been contrived in the eighteenth century to measure military engineers' mastery of the new trigonometry.

Around the world, there is an infrastructure gap between the walkable cities demanded by the carbon-conscious young and the road-heavy suburban developments built up over decades of automobility. There's a gap between the smart cities envisioned by computer programmers and the slow pace of state legislatures. Journalist Mike Davis might add the names of a thousand cities with over a million inhabitants in the developing world, most of them without effective sewerage, drinking water, or transportation systems. Around the world, infrastructure is creaking forward when it ought to be racing on the back of an information revolution.

We need new kinds of services that can pull together information to build the infrastructure of the future. Institutions that want to survive must concern themselves with the pragmatic questions of recruiting investors for resilient infrastructures. Consider the new financial investment packages such as those offered by the firm Hannon Armstrong over the last decade: these traders package sustainable infrastructure as a financial commodity in the hopes that investment can be driven by the market. Like

Fig. 8   Post office, London (Augustus Pugin Sr. and Thomas Rowlandson for Ackermann's Microcosm of London, 1808–11)

the Real Estate Investment Trusts of the 1970s on which they are modeled, infrastructure investment firms are designed to be flexible and fast enough to outpace slow government agencies and create new development along formulas never previously experimented with. If successful, they will mean that infrastructures of the future can be crowdfunded, opened to market wisdom and the swarming of possible investors who agree with a proposal.

Now, as in an earlier information revolution, new infrastructures happen from a hybrid of entrepreneurial spirit and the creative leveraging of funds. Consider the east–west rail corridor nearing completion through the diplomatic coordination of the United Nations, or the rapidly decreasing price of solar panels manufactured in India as the result of government protections for the industry. In our time, visionary forms of infrastructure like these depend upon the leveraging of government restrictions, standards, forms, certifications, and metrics—of coordinating information between massive lobbies, including designers, funders, and popular opinion.

There is, in our own time, a second infrastructure revolution afoot, one from below, that is even more powerful than the financial revolutions happening in the developed world. This is the participatory revolution in managing land and water at work in South America and India. From 1982 to 2006, developing-world activists used a process called "participatory mapping" to draw together a hundred people in a single village into a conversation about their infrastructure. Participatory mapping was used to design the formation of a local democratic consensus about water, sewers, irrigation works, and roads, as well as their maintenance, ownership, and use. These conversations emphasized democratic consensus around the best use of limited local resources, highlighting, for instance, traditional forms of rainwater harvesting for dry cities in India rather than ecologically inappropriate long-distance irrigation canals like those created since British rule by civil engineers. Participatory conversations drove forward new regimes of land and water management, including sustainable forestry management, a sanitation revolution in the developing world, rainwater harvesting, and experiments in participatory urban planning, many of which were being adapted by urban planners in the West by the late 1990s. Across the developing world, wherever participatory practices were installed, a revolution in information sharing transformed the way land and water were managed.

That information revolution was already powerful before the internet. Now, in the era of the smartphone, institutions like Stanford University and MIT are sending their graduate students to India and Tanzania to help promote participatory planning at a broad level. Cell phone mapping apps are used to manage land ownership in Mumbai's slums, to safeguard trees in Bangalore, to design a transport network in Kibera, and to envision a path network for a bikeable Moscow. Forged out of democratic consensus and the information of a mass public, these plans forecast the spread of a new kind of infrastructure, one designed to be resilient rather than to duplicate infrastructure designed for an era of cheap fuel. Participatory plans are more ambitious than traditional ones, targeting entire city-wide and regional land- and water-sheds, with the intention of benefiting the majority of the population (rather than the small segment represented by the tourist economy, the target of so many urban engineering projects in the developed world).

A revolution in information and a revolution in democracy together frame the possibility of a great rebuilding in the name of sustainability, of water and sanitation access for the masses. That era of rebuilding will not happen without a reorganization of human infrastructure—and flows of information—that is every bit as revolutionary as the eighteenth-century birth of civil engineering. Crowdmapping programs designed by information elites in India and Africa are coming up against the real limits of what can be done without broad access to GPS-enabled phones or nationwide satellite maps. Crowdsourcing and crowdfunding infrastructure at the scale of cities requires funders and visionaries to invest in the conditions of full participation: peer-to-peer sharing across national boundaries using the least effective technology. It requires fully funding a mass-training program for crowdsourced mapmaking and local infrastructure delivery. It means setting up an information infrastructure for sharing data about local property law on land and water. It requires setting up an information service online that encourages users to dream beyond mere questions of tourist dollars and employment to imagine a better economy, one rebuilt around safe and resilient drinking water and transportation for the next century. All of these forms of information sharing are viable in our time, but they require visionaries who can put together new information infrastructures with an eye to mobilizing investment and public attention to the rebuilding of cities.

Multifunctionality
to Exploit Redundancy

Malcolm Smith
Founding design director,
Integrated Urbanism Unit, and
global masterplanning
and urban design leader, Arup

Fig. 9

Malcolm Smith
(Judith Daniels, 2013)

Arup employs about eleven thousand people. It was founded by a Dane who was a philosopher, a mathematician, and an engineer. His enlightened gift to us was the idea that we can never own the company: we operate as a trust, a collective. We go in naked, and we come out naked. That's a scary thought for some people, but I think it's important as we talk about collaboration. Alexander [D'Hooghe] opened the session with an introduction to MIT, its departments, and their entrepreneurship. Among our eleven thousand people, there is an expectation of entrepreneurship. However, there is also a sense of the collective, a defaulting to the ability to operate as a whole. It goes deep down into our financial structure. I think that it is interesting, because we are professionals who practice in structures that allow us to create collective platforms of engagement.

I begin my discussion with the concept of a particular fossil that was pursued as the connecting piece between bird and sea evolution. This fossil is a fantasy. It was validated around the world, but then it became clear that it was constructed. I think the fantasy of the fossil, of hybridity joining together, is where we're going with infrastructure.

What I want to share with you today is a journey that starts where you may think we work and ends where you may be surprised we work. I think infrastructure and heavy engineering is an important, and continuing, part of the way the world works. In particular, I think of the high-speed link that the United Kingdom decided to build. Fifteen years after the Channel Tunnel was built and the French had constructed their high-speed rail line, the British government decided their high-speed route should go south of the Thames. We argued, in fact, that was the wrong place to put it: the route should go north of the Thames. Part of the reason was to open up connectivity to the north, so you didn't have to tunnel under the city. However, there was another story about some of the most deprived areas of the U.K. being disengaged and disenfranchised from the rest of Europe.

The British government then decided to place the route north of the river. Since then, a £5 billion investment has turned into a £30 billion-and-counting mobilization of capital, the Channel Tunnel Rail Link. Interestingly, that investment hasn't come from the government but from a private entity. The government chose the route and then handed over delivery of the system to that entity. They underwrote it, guaranteed it, but did not finance it. So, as the route comes into London, it enters a tunnel to mitigate. I think a continuing theme of heavy engineering, whether railroad or sewerage, is this denial that it actually exists. We're deep-burying systems, because we've got the technology, as Jo [Guldi] was talking about. At one moment we are inside the tunnel. And all of a sudden the rail pops out at a different place, Stratford in East London, the place that became the home of the Olympics. There's a story here about how this place was transformed. Through a simple diagram one can illustrate how, if you compress Europe relative to the time parameters of high-speed networks, the center is reformed. The Thames corridor of the U.K. becomes central. Its accessibility changes in a fundamental way.

It started on 178 acres (72 hectares) in Stratford, East London. Two-and-a-half million cubic meters of soil came out in order to dig tunnels and went onto the land, which raised it by eight meters out of a floodplain. It made the land, in one of the most deprived areas of the U.K., a new metropolitan center for this part of London. We did a master plan, and we created frameworks for development. There were actually fourteen million square feet (1,300,000 sq. m) of development planned here before people had even imagined London would host the Olympics. On the day of the announcement, I was sitting next to a member of Parliament. The message came from Singapore that the winner was London. The natural euphoria broke out, except for him. He was the under secretary to the treasury. He didn't move, so I turned to him and said, what's the issue? He said, "That wasn't supposed to happen. We weren't supposed to win it." I think the high-speed infrastructure was key to that, the accessibility, just seven minutes out of London. Taking the International Olympic Committee in Land Rovers through tunnels and popping out at St. Pancras Station. It was a remapping of place. It became something it couldn't become. So that's the physical infrastructure.

However, I share the view that infrastructure and monuments, both in terms of physicality and the outcomes they produce, are moving in a very different direction for us. Currently, we are examining a distributed network of energy and heat supply in London. Instead of taking four nuclear power stations and siting them around the outside of London, we are considering a whole system, done on a project-by-project basis, the resilience comes from the network and the integration of those systems. This idea being implemented could admittedly only come about with the reinstatement of the city-state, and that's the doing of the mayor of London. I think a critical issue going forward is the increasing role of the city as the state and politic in the delivery of infrastructure. Sitting inside of that energy and heat network is the Green Economic Zone, moving down through the Docklands, using devices, tools, and strategies to mobilize change. I think this is a powerful strategy, particularly in cities where some of the existing or redundant infrastructure can be used in a multitude of ways. What are the policies and devices that we apply to this infrastructure to move these changes forward?

Crossrail is the tunnel system that is going underneath London. London needs more capacity. It's a simple thing. However, the critical issue here is what this piece of infrastructure can do beyond the primary need. What we're investigating with Crossrail is taking the heat generated by trains deep in the ground and driving it back up into buildings. It's an efficient, optimized outcome for the train systems: they in turn become cooler, etc. However, it also creates a multiplicity of outcomes: a new income stream for the railway network, a new way it can engage the city, and a new way of actually operating. Finally, to stay in the tunnel mode, with heavy-lifting infrastructure, there is the Thames Tunnel. The tunnel is a new pipe that effectively runs under the river. We are remapping the river by creating this extra capacity for sewers. This fits with the interesting discussion about the overcapacity of infrastructure. London's first generation of infrastructure was in the embankments, at the edges of the city, and now we are driving it underneath. In these terms it is the beginning of a change in the way we relate to the environment and infrastructure, almost a denial of their need, a subversion of these conditions.

One of my roles is lead designer for the Southern District of the City of Amsterdam, the big commercial district, born of its accessibility to a highway, rail network, and Schiphol Airport, as well as of available land. In a way, it is its own worst enemy because of its beautiful view of water and landscape. There is an infrastructural corridor ripping through the middle of this successful but increasingly compromised development. So the city has taken the initiative. In spite of the tight economic parameters that the Netherlands, like everyone else, is experiencing, it has decided to lower about one and a half kilometers of road and railway system to enable the city to reconnect across this gap and to mitigate some of the air quality and acoustic issues. Currently, these issues create a monotony of use, but diversification can only happen with mitigation. Someone asked the nice question, Does the Netherlands always win, and is there always a good outcome? This wasn't one. The initial proposition was that this would all be done as one privately funded project. That collapsed. About four parties came to the table to continue this initiative. They named it the MLT, the mid- long-term project, in recognition that it is a stage in a process of project delivery that may stop. When one asks people to define longterm, they say, "Well, we'll get to midterm." There is no conclusion that it will move forward. However, with the building of this piece of infrastructure, there is the opportunity, as with Crossrail and other infrastructure that we're doing, to add in layers. These are two examples in Rotterdam: a water-collection system and a heat-recovery system in the road surface.

I want to move out of Europe for a while and talk about the beginning of de-engineering. Since 1940, Jeddah [Saudi Arabia] has grown into a burgeoning city, with its waterfront and harbor. When Jeddah was growing, two waterways were cut in to form quarries for city building. They were incised out of necessity, with no understanding of the hydrology. The waterways filled with stagnant sterilized water, exacerbated by the fact that the sewer system was leaching into the lagoons. We were asked to address solutions for the lagoons. One approach was to simply fill them in. The other opportunity was what we recommended, which was to try to locate a private development corporation to mobilize the 1,235 acres (500 hectares) of land here and to create this infrastructure. The story is simple. There is a one-square-kilometer lagoon and two parking systems that run into the lagoon. The tidal flow in this part of the Red Sea, about 2.5 to 3.3 feet (0.8 to 1 m), creates a natural flow system that takes water in and flushes the lagoon. In ten years, we could return the lagoons to the city by doing this, through a relationship between that piece of infrastructure and that development there. The plan opens up 7.5 miles (12 kilometers) of coastline and increases accessibility in the city.

My last two examples actually have nothing to do with physicality. My first example is Bethlehem in Palestine. Recently, a private initiative was set up in recognition that Bethlehem runs on considerable international development money. This money is being spent inappropriately, and Bethlehem is suffering significantly. An individual patron put forward the idea of creating the Bethlehem Development Initiative to work with the people of Bethlehem to set targets for development. There is a physical component to this, in understanding how these three small towns come together, adding up to a population of twenty-eight thousand people, and considering the constraints of where sewage can actually go. However, the two main issues, in terms of infrastructure, for which we're designing solutions now, are understanding the financing and governance strategies that enable the initiative to move forward. This isn't design in an architectural sense, but it is design in an enabling sense.

My second example is Pretoria in South Africa. The central area is actually hemorrhaging population, but it has a strong memory of the past. This is where Nelson Mandela was put on trial. This area suffers from the fact that over 40 percent of the economy is informal. It's how the city lives and thrives and trades. However, the inner area is dying; if anyone's been there, you know the dangers. Before the colonial government laid out a grid, there were two river systems that used to simply weave their way through the city. We have put forth a proposal for the reinstatement of this green *masanda*, a gathering place for the city in African culture. This green ring, this landscape of value, is part of a series of strategies related to land ownership and accessibility, so it's not just physicality that restructures the city in a different way.

My final example goes back to London. It's not about a big tunnel, or a big railway line. It's about an event twelve months before £10 billion of Olympic investment went on a television screen, and there were urban riots just up the road in Tottenham. Why in this part of London, this branded place, the home of the Tottenham Hotspurs football club? It seems to be the only brand that connects a diverse, challenged environment in inner London to the greater whole, which I think is a continuing condition. In response, we looked at many physical strategies. We determined accessibility was the critical one in relation to a transportation system for London that is concentric and fails to be localized. We're now working with Transport for London to redefine the first of what we call Zone Is, the local zones of catchment, so people can move within range of a financial and transport system of Transport for London and the College of Tottenham.

There are three things that I think are critical for us. One is the measurable systems. I heard what Stan [Allen] said, and I maybe do and maybe don't agree. I think the interrelationships of hard and soft infrastructure are the critical thing that we're trying to understand, the coefficients and how they marry with each other. There is no doubt as to the importance of software. I think the call to examine how the relationship between the physicality of design and the software of cities operates is absolutely paramount, if this cringe in regard to the role of the architect is to be addressed in a stronger and more confident way. How to address relocalization, this schizophrenic thing between centralized systems and relocalized systems, and finally, how to create the collective? This is a great challenge as we move forward. We can look, one, at the euphoria of sports events; two, at the interesting example of the declaration of the Apollo program; and three, at postdisaster strategy. How is the collective brought together and mobilized by the space of infrastructure? I want to finish with a drawing by a fourteen-year-old, from when we were working in Stratford. He drew a network of places in an experiential way that took away all the literalness of design, funding, all of that. It reminds me of the space that we have to occupy in the future.

5

confirming
the intermodal
station as
a viable
alternative

Establishing intermodal or interscalar exchange
points helps to maximize the potentials of intersecting networks. Connections between rail
and highway, parking and train, bus and subway, ship and truck increase the effectiveness
of each intersecting line. Furthermore, such
intersections form the de facto moments of
centrality in large dispersed metropolitan areas.
Markets have realized this and new development
wants to be near such intersections, but the critical missing piece—the design that
makes such spaces effectively connected on a pedestrian level and allows the val-
ue-add to occur—is missing. Conventional solutions from the historical city are often
inapplicable here because the scale and side effects (noise, pollution, vibration) of
the infrastructures in question preclude them. The participants in this chapter tackle
this critical missing piece.

marcel smets

petra todorovich
messick

stephen
crosby

cino
zucchi

Multimodal Infrastructure,
the Contemporary Monument

Marcel Smets
Professor of urbanism, Katholieke
Universiteit Leuven

Throughout history, networks have served to transport goods, facilitate travel, and engineer territorial organization. Successive eras have thus imprinted particular infrastructural systems upon their land of application. French absolutist powers built an encompassing system of canals in the seventeenth century to ship strategic goods and start a nationwide economy. The Enlightenment endorsed the implementation of a radial highway network in the second half of the eighteenth century, notably in France and the Austro-Hungarian Empire. Major cities were connected by straight-lined thoroughfares with a preset transversal profile—entitled "chaussées"—in order to smooth travel but also to lay down a hierarchy between cities. The Industrial Revolution that set off the urbanization in Europe and North America during the nineteenth century went hand in hand with the great development of railways. Toward the turn of the century, the expanding city limits required ever-growing public transport. Tramway or metro networks were established in response to passenger demand. With the introduction of the motorcar, urban extension was first based on parkways and later on motorways. In the 1950s the US National Highway System enlarged the prewar German example and set the standard for the interlinking motorways Europe constructed in the decades afterwards. In the second half of the twentieth century, the growth of international business and tourism provided for an intense network of commercial flights and an accumulation of airports all over the world. Once flying no longer proved competitive for shorter distances, Japan, China, and many European countries constructed their high-speed systems to sustain passenger transport along the corridors of intensive urbanization.

This overview, which basically reiterates common knowledge, shows an evolution of cycles in which the transport demand is predominantly met by a particular mode, usually triggered by a new technological development. These cycles overlap to some degree: the former cycle dies out during the period in which the new one starts up. Furthermore, the duration of each sequence tends to shrink as we move closer to our own age. During each of the cycles, the emphasis on the prevalent mode encourages the agents responsible for operating it to pay particular attention to the technology and management of this transportation network.

Such a narrow focus on the internal logic of the infrastructural system helps to explain the morphological detachment and self-centered functionality of most transportation networks. Every so often, they are conceived as an autonomous layer, independent of existing transport amenities and laid out following their own rationale. Optimizing their efficiency and return determines both the implantation of the lines and the position of the nodes (i.e., stations, airports). Connections between lines within the same system are seen in accordance to the hierarchy of the network structure: they make transfer possible and collect potential customers from origins served by subsidiary branches. In contrast to this frequent occurrence of intramodality, intermodality is usually scarce. It merely comes about when both transport modes can benefit from it, for example, in the case of interlinking bus and train stations that help to distribute passengers over the urban area of the station where the train arrives/departs, or in the provision of rail connections that give access to airports from major train stations or city centers.

An Operational Transport System Based on Existing Infrastructure

Several obstacles jeopardize the creation of new comprehensive transportation networks today. Their implementation would require the type of long-term vision and heavy investments, which are not present in times of economic difficulty. Furthermore, plans for new infrastructure are easily contested today. As a consequence, decision making gets to be so complex that they can hardly be brought to implementation. Playing on NIMBY reactions, lobbies nurtured by established transportation modes (e.g., petrol, car, and airline companies) often succeed in adequately opposing the introduction of new technologies. From this perspective, one cannot be but astonished to see how the HST [high-speed train] failed to be initiated in the North American urbanized corridors at a moment when China set out to build the most extensive TGV network in the world.

Evidence shows that digital connections become a substitute for real travel. Even if in some cases it appears that the growing number of e-relations also exerts in increase on passenger traffic, telephone and internet exchange also replace actual trips, especially in places where passenger transport is lengthy, uncomfortable, expensive, or insecure. In terms of business flows, e-technologies have previously led to forms of

delocalization that we would not have imagined possible. The long-term effect of electronic media on transport and travel probably needs more time to be correctly evaluated.

To be sure, we have many transportation networks already in existence. Some of them are only a shadow of what they used to be and would require deficient maintenance or substantial investment to improve their viability. But many networks are quite operational or would be with moderate improvements. In the period of scarcity that we are witnessing today—and predictions say for many years to come—these existing infrastructures could form the backbone of an more operational system. In order to do so, we need to improve the linkages between the present networks. The validity of this hypothesis needs to be verified for every particular case at hand. But practical evidence shows that the overall transport capacity in many cities and urban regions would be drastically enlarged if different modes interacted more fluently.

Multimodal Transfer as Keystone for Ubiquitous Accessibility

For that reason, realizing swift intermodal exchange appears to be the great challenge for the immediate future—not only in terms of transportation, but also in terms

Fig. 2   Regional LRT as a backbone for   Belgium (M. Blondia, E. De Deyn,
                the peri-urban landscape in 2050,   M. Smets, 2011)

of urbanity. If, as we suggest, money is generally lacking for constructing new transportation networks and if highways are getting increasingly saturated, the way to meet the expanding traffic demand is to make use of the residual capacity available in other modes of transportation. Such measures usually come down to intensifying cycling and making better use of public transport.

Paul Mees speaks about the Zurich Model: the Swiss city that, decades ago, overtly chose an intermodal approach—not only citywide but on the scale of its urban region—to guarantee accessibility to its major destinations in line with preserving their environmental quality. In order to do so, Zurich created a set of drastic traffic policies. It intensified the frequency of tram and bus lines, constructed the necessary missing links, put in place a unique fare for each public transport mode, and made the exchanges between them highly recognizable and user-friendly. In addition, it established elevated car park fees in central locations and systematically cut down on the space for automobile traffic when refurbishing road sections and giving priority to walking, cycling, and public transport. The result of this daring policy has proven enormously successful over the years: it re-established a balanced modal split for all daily trips within the Zurich agglomeration.

Daily life in Zurich displays evidence of the great advantages procured by such effective multimodal transport networks: ubiquitous accessibility, jobs, amenities, and services spread out over the city region. Banks, offices, department stores, the university, the main hospital, and even the zoo are situated in car-restricted areas. But the environmental and dwelling quality of these districts compensates for this limited car access to an extent that bankers and doctors, if they don't already live in the neighborhood, happily use the high-frequency tram to reach their workplaces.

Naturally, the Zurich Model doesn't lend itself to random replication. Even if other urbanized regions absolutely wanted to, they do not always have the lines in place to develop a citywide web of public transport. Neither may they have the means available, in this time of scarcity, for radically raising frequencies and spatially reorganizing the exchanges between public transport modes. Consequently, caution is necessary, but shouldn't prevent investigating the feasibility of multimodal accessibility in privileged corridors. Substantially lowering the number of car-oriented trips by intensifying public transport access along clustered strip developments might indeed constitute an important step to balance the modal split.

The Urban Value of Intermodal Change
Resorting to intermodal transfer generates stepping stones for enhanced urban activity. By definition, the multimodal web produces a hierarchy of nodal points, depending on the number and importance of lines that constitute them. It produces a rating in the central character of the surrounding areas, which in turn leads to differentiation in urban mix and composition. In contrast with customary intramodal exchanges (extended train stations or bus terminals in peripheral locations), where movement and activity are encapsulated within the enclosures of a built facility, the great attraction of intermodal transfer lies in its innate relationship to the public sphere. In fact,

the passage between modes takes place either in a nondistinct setting, mutualized between transport providers, or in a public walkway between two terminals. Unlike a station or terminal, it is not reserved for passengers, and for that reason intermodal transfer contributes to enlivening the public realm.

On the other hand, multimodal transfer points do not just create flows of people. The movement of passengers they facilitate forms an important reason for other activities to settle. Commerce and services depend on customers passing by who increase the liveliness of the space. Services initially based on a transport-generated clientele expand conveniences addressed to citizens at large. But transfer points also develop as central places for inhabitation and job provision. They become places of aggregation and densification around stops of (light) rail or tramway—sometimes looking like village nuclei of transport oriented development but more often like articulations within a more or less continuous urban structure, identifying districts by the specific character of agglomerated activities around the intermodal stop.

An Object for Multidisciplinary Research
If MIT's Center for Advanced Urbanism is intended to contribute to civic improvement through multidisciplinary and design-oriented research, developing models for intermodal networks and detailing schemes for effective and inspiring ways to realize multimodal transfer in many different contexts obviously meets the purpose. In terms of transport and mobility studies, such an endeavor might turn out to be one of the most meaningful entries into today's reality: a task that certainly fulfills the goals of top engineers—namely, to increase the quality of daily life in a sustainable way.

High-Speed Rail as Driver for New Multimodal Developments

Petra Todorovich Messick
Senior officer of outreach and
communications, Northeast Corridor
Infrastructure and Investment
Development, Amtrak

The Northeast Corridor Infrastructure Investment and Development Division of Amtrak focuses primarily on the management of the infrastructure of the Northeast Corridor, from Boston to New York to Washington, D.C. That line, which serves about a third of our national ridership, and carries a great deal of regional rail traffic as well, is the largest asset that Amtrak owns. We have a very large management responsibility with that corridor infrastructure, including all the bridges, signaling systems, overhead electrical wires, and so forth. One question that I was thinking about in putting this presentation together, and really that our Northeast Corridor Infrastructure Investment Development Group grapples with every day, is, How do we retrofit and upgrade a one-hundred-year-old railroad for the twenty-first century? Furthermore, in the context of this panel, where we are looking beyond the Northeast Corridor, another key question is, Is the model that we have in the Northeast—which is densely developed for the United States and has a great variety of station types and many intermodal stations—a model that can be applied to other parts of the country? If not, what is the approach? What role do intermodal stations play in other parts of the country where there are different types of regional land development patterns?

At Amtrak, we see the intermodal station in the Northeast megaregion as a fact of life. I say this because of our land-use patterns. Considering population density in the Northeast as if in the form of three-dimensional heat maps, one will find wonderful peaks of density in Manhattan, Boston, Philadelphia, Baltimore, and D.C. These land development patterns grew up around the investments made in the intercity rail corridor over one hundred years ago. The regional rail systems in New York, Boston, Philadelphia, Baltimore, and D.C. bring people, on a daily basis, from the surrounding suburbs to the hub, the central business district, to conduct business and have face-to-face interactions. As we look into the twenty-first century, I believe these face-to-face interactions will remain a vital center of our economy in the United States and globally. At the turn of the century, we thought that maybe technology would change things. People will work from home more, they have their wireless devices, they don't need face-to-face interactions as much. While that has happened, and people are more mobile and can work from wherever they are, I think the face-to-face interactions that rely on transportation infrastructure and networks coming together have become even more important in our economy. We find that most high-value jobs in the Northeast rely on these type of interactions taking place. And we see it happening because we made these investments and overbuilt heavy-rail infrastructure over one hundred years ago. Today, that investment sustains an incredible density and vitality of economic interaction that goes on day in and day out.

The work that I was doing before I came to Amtrak was with the Regional Plan Association, a nonprofit civic organization in New York. There, I was running the America 2050 initiative, a national program focused on the need for infrastructure investment. We were doing a lot of research on the promise of high-speed rail in the United States and what the approach should be to locating high-speed rail stations in the context of different land uses. One of the studies for our report, "High Speed

Rail in America," looked at the population density in each of the five largest cities in the Northeast and the layers of local transit, regional rail, and intercity rail on which these cities and regions depend. The statistics suggest that over 70 percent of the heavy rail ridership in the United States is concentrated in these Northeastern cities. So I don't think you can overstate the important role that these infrastructure systems and networks play in our economy in the Northeast. I think they will continue to be an advantage if we can maintain them in good repair. That's the challenge that my colleagues and I now grapple with at Amtrak, because we're always operating in a funding-constrained environment.

I think I've made the case that in the Northeast, we have a lot of intermodal stations, and they play a very real and important role in our economy. We really

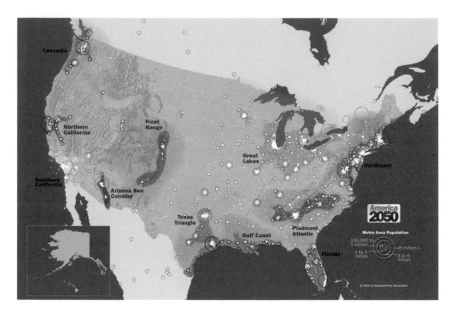

use transit. But what about the rest of the country where you have very different land-development types? In fact, the majority of development in the United States is suburban. My answer to that is, let's look at the megaregions in the United States. A few years ago, when there was debate over the president's high-speed rail program, I heard many critics say that high-speed rail can never work in the United States because we're too decentralized: the country is too big, and the distances are too large. It's important to clarify that we shouldn't be talking about linking the coasts with high-speed rail. High-speed rail works optimally across distances of 150 to 600 miles (241 to 966 km), at the upper limits, to connect proximate hubs or proximate metropolitan areas. You can find these proximate metropolitan regions in the ten or eleven megaregions identified through research in recent years. For example, this

Fig. 4

The Regional Plan Association's America 2050 Initiative identifies eleven megaregions in the United States, where 70 percent of the nation's population and jobs are located. (America 2050, a program of Regional Plan Association) map shows eleven megaregions in the country. These megaregions are networks of metropolitan areas connected by business travel, overlapping commuting patterns, linked economies, shared history and culture, to some extent, and large natural areas. They're a useful planning framework for thinking about large systems that span hundreds of miles, like high-speed rail and electricity-transmission networks, as well as large natural landscapes that stretch across multiple states.

That being said, when we look at Amtrak's ridership throughout the country—and I just pulled a snapshot of our ten busiest train stations in the country—they still are mostly in the Northeast, on the West Coast, and in Chicago. These are the busiest places where people are getting on and off trains, and where we have the best train service. We also have long-distance services, which are much less frequent and reliable, partially because these are services that we operate on freight corridors that we don't own or control.

If you look at different regions, the approach to rail stations, as Marcel [Smets] pointed out, is very nodal. There is a station in one place, and you really have to pick where it is. The report "High Speed Rail in America" demonstrates two potential approaches to locating a station, in two very different regions of similar population size. Houston and Philadelphia are each regions of six million people. Population density in Philadelphia is concentrated within a two-mile ring. Within two miles (3.2 km) of the city center, there are about 220,000 people residing. In Houston, you have 72,000 people within two miles of the center. At the ten-mile (16-km) ring, there are about 2.1 million people in Philadelphia, and 1.5 million in Houston. By the time you get out to the 25-mile (40-km) ring, it's virtually the same. So, two similar-sized cities, but the population is distributed differently. For anyone who's been to these two cities, the differences are quite evident. In Philadelphia, it's quite obvious where the station should go. It exists at the hub of many regional connections. But in Houston, there needs to be a different approach for an intermodal station, particularly a high-speed rail station. It must be connected to the highway network, because that's how the majority of Houstonians get around, and it's probably going to have to provide considerable amounts of parking. It must also be connected to new investments that are taking place in that city, like the light-rail station. We have to really think about the opportunity for more distributive networks in Houston.

I pulled an image from the California High Speed Rail Authority's website, showing their station plans for Anaheim, to demonstrate the kind of location decision required in more decentralized and auto-based environments like Anaheim. This is the authority's plan for the ARTIC Station, or Anaheim Regional Transportation Intermodal Center. Here, you have high-speed regional rail connections, local light rail, connections with the highway system, and thousands of parking spaces. It does pose the question, Do you get the same environmental and economic benefits that you might get from a high-speed rail station when you provide so much room for parking, when you use so much surface area at a station location for that use? However, I think that the California planners would argue that it's necessary for the ridership, to make the system work. This is all to point out that different regional land development types require different approaches to the intermodal station.

I also want to go quickly refer to a typology of high-speed rail stations in Europe that I developed with the Lincoln Institute of Land Policy, here in Cambridge.

In particular, I want to point out a station in Leida, Spain. The entire study looked at forty different high-speed rail stations in France and Spain and extracted from them different approaches. We saw Leida as an ideal case study. When the high-speed rail system was built in Spain, the city retrofit the historic station for high-speed rail and, in doing so, bridged over the tracks that had created a seam in the urban fabric between the historic center and the more industrial area of town that was transitioning into a new center. High-speed service put them within two hours of Madrid and one hour of Barcelona, causing an uptick in business and tourism travel, economic development, and tourist dollars spent in the city. They really have reaped the benefits of the new station, because they were thoughtful about linking it to the historic urban

fabric and other transportation modes. In contrast, we also looked at Avignon—and Marcel probably knows more about this case study than I do, due to his familiarity with France—where the high-speed rail station is really on the outside of town, separate from the historic center. Because of this location, the station sort of exists in tension

Fig. 5   California's Proposed Anaheim   Center (California High Speed Rail
              Regional Transportation Intermodal   Authority)

with the conventional rail station in the center of town. Since it was built in a flood plain, there are no plans for surrounding development. It really is a special-purpose site that requires a bus transfer or driving to get there. As a result, it has not really flourished from an economic development prospective or generated the same sort of ancillary benefits as in the case of Leida.

With regard to stations, in 2008 the United States passed a rail bill called the Passenger Rail Investment Improvement Act, which set the course for a new approach to rail in the United States. It included steadier funding for Amtrak and new policies to assist with the management of Northeast Corridor infrastructure, like a fairer distribution of payment between the commuter-rail agencies and the infrastructure owner, Amtrak. Immediately after that, with the election of President Obama and the passage of the stimulus bill, about $10 billion in funding was pumped into high-speed

rail. These two events brought in a new era for rail in this country, after many years of struggling to just keep the Northeast Corridor infrastructure in good condition and keep the railroad running. Under those pressures, stations were often seen as a liability, and we tried to minimize responsibilities for them. Now, there's been a sea change. At Amtrak, within the group I work for, we are now looking toward the future and recognizing the importance of these assets for the future of the Northeast economy and the entire United States. That's a long way of saying that, while we used to not have any plans for our major stations in the Northeast Corridor, now we do. We are actively involved in major planning efforts for them.

I'm going to talk briefly about Union Station in Washington, D.C. However, there are plans underway for Boston's South Station, led by the Massachusetts Department

Fig. 6   Aerial perspective of the proposed air rights development and transformed Washington Union Station   (Akridge and Shalom Baranes Architects)

of Transportation, as well as plans for New York Penn Station, Baltimore Penn Station, and Philadelphia's Thirtieth Street Station. We see these stations as important civic spaces and places for the future. In Washington, D.C., like Leida, the rail yards create a sort of seam in the urban fabric. Washington's been somewhat of a victim of its own success in that the city is undergoing a revitalization, with exciting new neighborhoods like NoMa that are growing very fast. Ridership has gone up, and the station is at capacity. The tracks are outdated, the passenger experience is frustrating, and a lot needs to be done. Our plan is to remove the existing parking garage that's over the tracks, reconfigure the tracks, expand the concourse level, and complete a real estate overbuild on a platform over the station. Essentially, the result will be a new configuration of tracks and platforms. The First Street level provides new connections to the neighborhood, a new train shed, and air-rights development, in partnership with the Akridge Development Company in Washington, D.C. The project includes about three million square feet of mixed-use development on the platform over the rail yards. H Street, currently a bridge over the rail tracks, will be at the same level as this new development. Thus, the changes are reuniting different parts of the city and even providing visual linkages to the capitol.

In closing, I want to reinforce the fact that stations are hubs. They are places that bring people together to do their work in a face-to-face environment on a daily basis. The different regional land-use approaches across the country require different responses to creating stations. In the Northeast, our challenge is retrofitting existing infrastructure, which requires service disruptions, property acquisition and consolidation, and a lot of money. In contrast, in more decentralized regions, there may be more greenfield development. You may have more opportunity to acquire property and build new infrastructure, but you lack the benefits of density and existing intermodal connections. Both are very worthy pursuits and deserve our attention, despite their differences.

The Pioneering Role of Logistics in the Development of Multimodal Platforms

Stephen Crosby
President, CSX Real Property, Inc.

Fig. 7

Stephen Crosby
(Ana Vargas, 2013)

The term *intermodalism*, while used across many disciplines, has been most commonly used, lately, in the freight-rail context. And, as I'll show you, the American intermodal model is the best in the world for moving freight.

With that, I'm going to start with a quick discussion of the supply chain. Alex [Klatskin] talked about the supply chain and showed the port in New York which is similar to what I'll discuss. Things get manufactured in Asia, as he said, and they come to U.S. ports and get put on trains or trucks. If they are put on trains, they go to an inland rail terminal, which is generally called an intermodal terminal, and then get put on trucks and delivered to warehouses, stores, or even houses. So that's how a supply chain works in the context of freight railroading in the United States. There are 160,000 miles (257,495 km)—and I'm going to counter one of the speakers this morning with this point—of privately owned railroad rights-of-way in the United States. In fact, by and large, U.S. railroad rights-of-way are privately owned. The Northeast Corridor is probably the one major exception in this regard. There are lots of local lines, like the T, that are publicly owned. However, the major freight infrastructure in this country is private. I would say the same for the pipeline system that you saw. These are not government-owned rights-of-way, they are private rights-of-way. The electric utility lines that you see everywhere are also privately owned rights-of-way. Thus, our ability to capture these rights-of-way for any use is going to be limited by the fact that ownership is not in common. It doesn't mean that can't happen, and there are many examples where cohabitation of rights-of-way does occur. However, I wanted to clear that up before I went further.

Proximity to the 160,000 miles (257,495 km) of rail lines across the country has been a key driver for our economy. It is why most of our freight moves by rail. Since 1980, the private railroads have invested over $525 billion of private money to lay new track, purchase equipment, and maintain bridges and equipment. Railroads spend about five times as much capital on their business as the next most capital-intensive industry in the country. So it's a very expensive, capital-intensive business. It's also one that, fortunately, in this country, we've been able to figure out how to pay for using private means.

Rail is the most efficient means of moving freight on land. Moving freight by water is the cheapest way to move freight. This is why there is all this discussion about the Panama Canal expansion, because the freight will stay on a ship longer if it's coming from China and going to the East Coast and therefore should be a little cheaper. However, that's going to depend on the toll that Panamanians charge to use their new canal, and that's yet to be determined. So we'll see how that works. The Environmental Protection Agency estimates that every ton of freight that moves by rail instead of by truck on the highway reduces greenhouse emissions by approximately two thirds. That's important. Rail-truck intermodal, the combination of rail to cover the distance and a truck for pickup and delivery, is the most efficient means of moving containerized freight any distance over five hundred miles (805 km) across land. The Federal Railroad Administration has also stated that the U.S. freight rail system is the safest, most efficient, and most cost-effective in the world. They are a safety organization, not a commercial organization, and so they're not saying this in a self-serving way but based on what their research has indicated. Rail is also an extremely efficient means of moving people, as Petra [Todorovich Messick] said, usually across shorter distances. Even the high-speed distances that she discussed are much shorter than the average freight distance. The Northeast Corridor is another great example of heavy rail being used to move people. The Boston subway system, the T, is a great example of light rail being used to move people very effectively.

All these examples align appropriate infrastructure with a need to be addressed. I want to say that again. The appropriateness of the infrastructure relative to the need is crucial. I think you'll see this theme come up again and again. So I want to give you a few examples of what that might look like. Heavy-haul rail systems, as I said, are generally privately owned. They combine network design, car design, locomotive design, and sizing to enable us to move a ton of freight about five hundred miles (805 km) on a gallon of diesel fuel. You may have heard some ads—our company has sponsored some of them—but it's really true: there's significantly greater efficiency in using rail to move freight. Rail-truck intermodal, as I said before, also runs on a privately owned network. It combines a more sophisticated network infrastructure and dedicated facilities, including specially built loading and unloading terminals. It also depends on the local road network for freight to move effectively. For example, freight can move from Chicago to New York, or Chicago to Boston, by intermodal transport in about forty-six hours. The freight company picks up the goods at a warehouse or manufacturer by truck, takes them to the terminal, puts them on the train for 46 hours, takes them off the train, puts them on the truck, and takes them to a warehouse or a distribution point. Thus, in a shade over two days, you've gone from loading dock to loading dock, Chicago to Boston, and you just can't do that as efficiently any other way. As Alex said, this stuff is really big, it's loud—all of those things are true—and to make these systems work, you need them to be in the right place, built the right way, with the right technology.

So here's what we're talking about: five hundred acres of rail and pavement, massive infrastructure. Each container is roughly forty feet (12.2 m) long, eight feet (2.4 m) wide, and ten or twelve feet (3.1 or 3.7 m) tall; a crane has a span over one hundred feet (30.48 m). There are five of them at our sorting hub in the middle of a cornfield in Ohio, where trains from the west meet trains from the east. It's like the Atlanta airport, a great big hub, where cargo is transferred very quickly and efficiently. The Northeast Corridor is another well-designed piece of infrastructure, designed to move people on a different kind of scale. Again, it's very appropriate for its use. The D.C. subway is a great example of another type of rail.

Another thing: when people see a railroad track, they just think, "There's a railroad track." However, there's actually five or six different levels of service that can occur on tracks, and they can't all occur at the same time. You may have noticed that the high-speed tracks that you saw in Petra's pictures were generally out of town, or connected with a bypass to go into town. The curvature and alignment needed to run a high-speed train are extremely different from for a subway train or the T, which can twist underneath, or a freight train, which lumbers along at forty miles an hour (64 km an hour) versus 240 (385 km an hour). I think about it this way: The country lane or the subdivision street with two lanes is made out of asphalt, and so is the interstate highway with eight lanes. If you didn't use them all the time, they might seem like the same thing. Railroad tracks are similar. They can be the neighborhood street or the Interstate Highway System. So, when you design an intermodal station, it's critical to understand the modes that will be there. But I'm getting ahead of myself. The message here is, make sure that you understand the systems that you're trying to connect, and make sure they're appropriate for the purposes that you're trying to achieve in your station.

In order for rail systems to be effective for people or freight, they have to provide regular and reliable service, and support viable markets. Viable markets are something I think that Alex and Don [Briggs] mentioned. However, viable markets frequently don't enter the station-design conversation. So, viable systems and viable markets are critical to a working station. How do we translate this idea into a passenger version of intermodalism? The success of the intermodal station will be directly tied to the transportation service it supports and the market it serves—no network, no market, no success. Combining the right services with the appropriate infrastructure to support the services is critical. If you choose the wrong mix of modes, or build inappropriate infrastructure to support those modes, such as putting a local transit system on a freight track with an intermodal station nearby, it probably won't work because you won't get the reliable transit service you need to serve the market that you believe is there. Every mode requires its own unique infrastructure, and every market metro is going to be different, so one size is not going to fit all. That's going to be a problem, different because top-down federal programs are not likely to be successful, unless the rules are very flexible. Someone mentioned flexibility this morning. It really is key.

In some cases, the intermodal station will only serve a hub-and-spoke role, like the facility in Ohio. John F. Kennedy International Airport is an example of that kind of facility in the airport world. It serves international travelers and people across the country, but it doesn't necessarily serve the local market, other than to get travelers to Europe. In other cases, an intermodal station is going to be a destination that serves multiple modes. The PATH station in the old World Trade Center is a great example. Finally, in some other cases, it can serve both of these purposes, like Union Station in Washington, D.C.—the current one, not even the future one—and be both a hub and a destination. In a hub-and spoke-model, network connectivity and network density are the drivers. It's about quickly consolidating and redistributing the people or freight that you're moving. It doesn't require much ancillary development to be effective. However, ancillary development can occur, so that you get both the successful destination and the successful flow-through of people and/or freight. Think about how critical the last mile is for freight. If UPS didn't have the brown trucks, it couldn't get to your door. UPS is our company's largest customer. Everybody thinks of it as a truck company, but they use rail very heavily. The brown truck provides the last mile and drives the success of that business.

Let's look at another example: the proposed high-speed rail line between Orlando and Tampa in Florida. It was part of the stimulus program. However, the governor of Florida gave the money back. Why? The right-of-way for this project is terrific. It's in the middle of [Interstate] I-4, at a separated grade, so it doesn't have any conflicts. It goes from downtown Tampa to downtown Orlando. It was shovel ready, which is why it became part of the stimulus program. The problem is that neither Orlando nor Tampa has good public infrastructure. They have nothing linking downtown to the suburbs, so there's no ability for high-speed connectivity to serve the market because you have to get in your car to reach the high-speed rail. Once you get in your car, you might as well drive to Tampa, because there's no reason to get in your car from a suburb of Orlando, drive to downtown Orlando, get out of the car, get on the high-speed train, and then rent a car in Tampa, because wherever you're going is not connected to anything either. It doesn't make any sense. The high-speed rail was a very good idea, but the timing was bad: the cart just got before the horse. And I support the governor in what he did in that particular case.

So what does this experience tell us? It tells us that "build it and they will come" is not the best strategy. We need to understand where the density of people will occur from a market perspective. We need to build a dense and reliable multimodal transit system to serve it. We need to assemble the rights-of-way necessary to provide longer-distance connectivity, so when it is time to connect Orlando and Tampa, we'll have a way to do it. Finally, we need to preserve and/or relocate the current infrastructure that's serving us well, so that it can continue to serve us well in the future. From my perspective, that means not putting local transit on the freight-railroad tracks.

Public Spaces for the Multimodal Fragment

Cino Zucchi
Partner,
Cino Zucchi Architetti

Fig. 8

West view, Bozen Rail Areal
Competition "Arbo," Bozen,
Italy, 2010 (Cino Zucchi Architetti
with Plan Team, Park Associati,

D. Tumioti, Evitec S.A.S., CZA,
Geoproject, Maxmakers, Space
Syntax, WSP UK, Avv. Dr. Karl
Zeller, 2010)

Bozen Rail Area Competition
The proposal for the redesign of the station area and the spaces vacated by the railway tracks in Bozen [Italy] needed to respond to a number of concrete needs expressed by the city while resolving the challenges presented, as well as the potential expressed by its urban history: a city where the relationship with the impressive

surrounding landscape of the valley and the mountains is both a significant historical limit and a significant resource. Contemporary culture and its renewed sensibility toward the environment has activated urban and landscape design tools in a more sophisticated way, providing richness and variety to new areas of the city, and integrating their different parts with the surrounding landscape, while considering urban centers as part of a larger system where urban and natural environments can find a new equilibrium. The proposal is configured as a "graft" where the elements of the railway system—the new road network, the public spaces, the proposed new urban fabrics, the river and its bridges, the structure of the public mobility, and the green network—are integrated with the existing city, projecting it into a new urban and natural dimension: a real "sustainable urbanism" that combines urban intensity and environmental quality, and reduces private traffic. Two major green inserts bring the surrounding green landscape into the city, giving form to the proposed new urban fabrics. The new road network continues and complements the existing one, multiplying the connections between the parts and creating a simple structure of paths that supports the new intervention. Around this double frame of roads and green spaces, the sites of the new buildings are configured as porous elements, in continuous dialogue with the open spaces and with the existing parts of city, to render the difference in scale between new and old almost invisible. The mix of existing houses, offices, and industrial buildings is completed and complemented by a series of new buildings and spaces of high environmental quality, generating a widespread redevelopment that can recognize and appreciate both the differences and the connections between the parts.

The artifact of the new station is envisaged more as a geographic rather than a technical element; a large photovoltaic canopy suspended above the tracks with a

Fig. 9	View of the new station, Bozen Rail Areal Competition "Arbo," Bozen, Italy, 2010 (Cino Zucchi Architetti with Plan Team, Park Associati,	D. Tumiati, Evitec S.A.S., CZA, Geoproject, Maxmakers, Space Syntax, WSP UK, Avv. Dr. Karl Zeller, 2010)
Fig. 10	Model of Bozen Rail Areal Competition "Arbo," Bozen, Italy, 2010(Cino Zucchi Architetti with Plan Team, Park Associati,	D. Tumiati, Evitec S.A.S., CZA, Geoproject, Maxmakers, Space Syntax, WSP UK, Avv. Dr. Karl Zeller, 2010)

series of skylights that look onto the Rosengarten mountain complex, traces with its sharp broken profile the visual skyline for two new plazas: one for trams and regional trains toward the historic center and one for the bus station toward the south and the river. A pedestrian ramp located near the office building of the province gently connects the north square to the new bus station on the south. A cluster of mixed-use towers overlooks this new plaza, interacting with the new building around Via del Macello and even more with the steep slopes of the Virgolo.

Temporary environmental screens at the entrance of the Vedeggio-Cassarate tunnels are "wounds" inflicted on geology to facilitate human movements. Their history is ancient, glorious, and gory, but today techniques have been refined to the point of making the excavation similar to keyhole surgery. The new Vedeggio-Cassarate tunnel that connects the Lugano stadium neighborhood to the Milan–Zurich highway has

already triggered an extensive urban transformation of the area, which will become the new entrance point to the city from the north. Pending the completion of the link with the existing road, the entrance and exit from the tunnel on the Cassarate side require a temporary arrangement that would blend with the surrounding landscape while screening the structural work under construction: that of a large pedestrian walkway serving as a sound barrier that will connect the new upper park to the river.

The project is based on a simple idea—namely, the repetition of a series of sprucewood poles of varying lengths, creating a cinematic sculpture by the formal resources of parametric design programs. A "grooved surface" (the geometric definition of a curved surface obtained with rectilinear sections that rotate in space) moves to reflect the geographical limits and the dynamic vision of those driving by. A large sinuous

Fig. 11

View from the inside of the gallery, works of environmental mitigation at the entrance of the Gallery Vedeggio-Cassarate, Lugano,

Switzerland, 2011–2012 (Cino Zucchi Architetti with Mauri & Banci SA, 2011–2012)

"screen" reaching heights of thirty-three feet (10.1 m) and undulating between concave and convex forms—at times permeable, at times opaque, depending on the driver's point of view—constitutes a kind of environmental sculpture emphasizing the entrance to the city from the highway.

A parterre of white pebbles conceals the point where the cantilevered poles enter the ground, allowing structural details to disappear in favor of existing ground levels through a continuous sequence of open spaces of different qualities. The detailed plan for the tower area is developed in line of with the spatial hypothesis contained in the outline plan and takes into consideration the wishes of the city planning committee by advocating slender mixed-use towers. The plan for the tower area gives functional and spatial substance to the longer sequence of strategic decisions about the future of the area and its relationship with the wider urban framework.

The fabric of tower buildings envisaged by the plan, around an open area of high architectural quality, is distinguished by the fact that every tower features a combination of offices on the lower floors and residences on the upper ones. Both on an urban-design level and an architectural one, the project pays considerable attention to the issue of energy saving and environmental sustainability in the new city—with the contribution of BuroHappold—in relation to the latest technical innovations and materials in the area. Connections across the site are strongly related with the understanding of existing and future infrastructures. Roads, bike paths, pedestrian walkways, train station, tramways, and the planned metro station, as well as the proposed retail development to happen north of the bridge, are carefully considered by the scheme. The limited number of parking areas provided is also part of the overall transport strategy, allowing for a well-balanced supply of public and private infrastructures.

The project, which can at this point in time be considered the most significant in the transformation of the Finnish capital, has met considerable success with the public and with the administration and operators in the sector, and represents an innovative contribution to the question of how design can respond to new environmental issues of energy conservation, traffic efficiency, and socially stimulating urban hubs. The existing bridge, which was the only connection between the two urban quarters on the two sides of the existing "infrastructural valley" represented by the railway yard, has been transformed into a lively urban area by redefining its northern edge and extending the existing atrium of the station into a covered collective space hosting new commercial functions and responding to Helsinki's cold climate.

Fig. 13   View from northeast, detailed plan of the Central Pasila Tower area, Helsinki, Finland, 2009 (Cino Zucchi Architetti with OneWorks, BuroHappold London, 2009)

6

in memoriam: manuel de solà-morales, city choreographer

In September 2012 Manuel de Solà-Morales passed away. He placed infrastructure design on the agenda for urbanists, architects, and engineers in Europe, and he has inspired at least two generations of designers. Because of this important legacy, the Center for Advanced Urbanism organized a competition for an installation to celebrate his work and, during the "Infrastructural Monument" conference, exhibited the built winning project by architecture student Erioseto Hendranata. This volume concludes with a reflection on Solà-Morales's work.

lorena bello
gomez

City Choreographer

Lorena Bello Gomez
Lecturer, Department of Architecture,
Massachusetts
Institute of
Technology

Fig. 7   Presenting a selection of publica-   conference, 2013
tions by Manuel de Solà-Morales   (Judith Daniels, 2013)
at the Infrastructural Monument

Manuel de Solà-Morales i Rubió, one of the most important architects and urban thinkers of the last quarter of the twentieth century and the beginning of the twenty-first, died in Barcelona—the city that served as the laboratory for his urban research and praxis—on February 27, 2012. He passed away at the age of seventy-three, but his sound lessons and rich legacy on the matter of city thinking and making will guide

generations of designers in the decades to come. Solà-Morales's intellectual discourse gave us the tools and grammar to tackle, maneuver, and sculpt the urban matter of the city: *com fer ciutat*. His urban projects at the intermediate scale, between the urban plan and architecture, always found a recurrent point of departure and inspiration in the intersection of architecture, public space, and infrastructure. In particular, designers will remember his investigation of the relationship of city and sea through urban port projects in many European cities.

To honor Solà-Morales's memory, on the one-year anniversary of his death, the recently launched MIT Center for Advanced Urbanism (CAU) announced a design competition for its first inaugural symposium, the raison d'être of this publication, where students from the School of Architecture + Planning at MIT were asked to interpret one of Solà-Morales's best infrastructural projects. The winning proposal, Kinetic Infrastructure, submitted by my teaching assistant at the time, Erioseto Hendranata, abstracted the serpentine and meandering nature of Solà-Morales's latest waterfront project, the Scheveningen Boulevard in The Hague, the Netherlands, as a frontage in a constant dialogue with the ever-changing seafront environment, and translated these qualities into an intriguing artifact that Solà-Morales would have enjoyed himself.

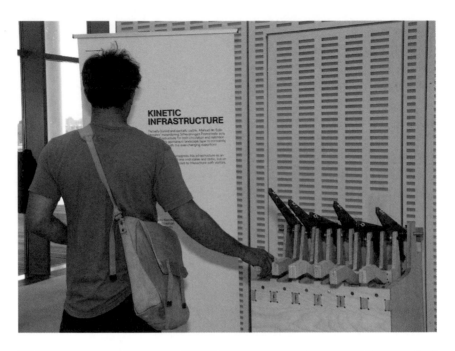

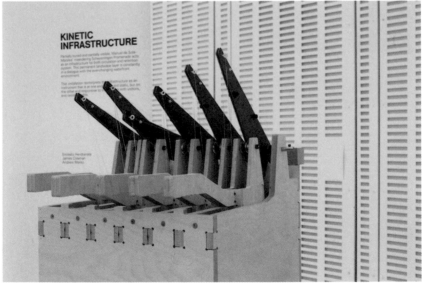

Fig. 2	The winning entry of the Infrastructural Monument competition commemorated one of the greatest infrastructural designers	of the past decade: Manuel de Solà-Morales (Judith Daniels, 2013)
Fig. 3	Kinetic Infrastructure was designed by Erioseto Hendranata, with assistance from James Coleman	and Andrew Manto (Lorena Bello Gomez)

With this designed memorial, the CAU linked itself to a network of events in Europe and the Americas that honored Solà-Morales's sound career with publications like the *D'UR* farewell issue, which gave voice to his long list of friends and colleagues and the symposium "Roots for a Twenty-First Century Urbanism" hosted by the Harvard Graduate School of Design. The latter explored Solà-Morales's vision to cast light onto new contemporary urban problems through the glances of unconditional friends and collaborators. All in all, these tributes captured a brilliant and generous personality, even if the constraints of an essay, a symposium, or even a volume such as this one would not do full justice to it.

I have no doubt that Solà-Morales would have been very pleased with the Infrastructural Monument Symposium and this publication's acknowledgement of the power and potential of his ideas about infrastructure for an always-evolving urban

condition. I would like to use this opportunity to announce his soon-to-be opened archive at the Collegi d'Arquitectes de Catalunya in Barcelona, formed by his more than four thousand books and writings that have been donated by his generous companion Rosa Feliu. This life archive, formed by volumes frequently signed by its authors thanking Solà-Morales for his contributions or inspiration to the publication, will allow many scholars to continue his most prolific and passionate life project: the study and design of cities.

More than a jewel of knowledge, Solà-Morales's library is the most telling example of his multifaceted approach to the understanding of urbanity and places, which he studied through the lens of architecture. However, Solà-Morales might have employed a lens of geography, as he has recognized in many occasions, had

Fig. 4   Manuel de Sola-Morales's Archive
                at the COAC in Barcelona
                (Lorena Bello Gomez)

his father and grandfather not been renowned Catalan architects. In his thorough analysis of sites, where nothing is taken for granted, Solà-Morales employs rigorous scans through the work of urbanism's related arts and sciences, whether through the glances of a filmmaker like Éric Rohmer or Michael Winterbottom, an economist like John Maynard Keynes, an urban historian like Joseph Rykwert, a philosopher-sociologist like Henri Lefebvre or Richard Sennett, a geographer like David Harvey or Neil Smith, a photographer like Manolo Laguillo, a cultural critic such as Fredric Jameson or a great soccer player like Johan Cruyff.

Solà-Morales believed that through these scans, filtered by drawing and mapping, the urbanist could transform himself into a wanderer and detective who frames the clues and potentials of the site. Only then would the design response become a synthetic topography with potential to give a universal answer in architectonic terms

and effects beyond its area of intervention, as a needle does in acupuncture. Such a process escapes foreseeable and predictable answers, as it starts with no prejudices or preconceptions, and seeks opportunity where others only find problems, just by changing the way we look at things as he did with the periphery of cities. Through Solà-Morales's approach, the project not only gives a solution to the site, in the normal three-dimensional manner through its section, but more importantly, has the potential to affect the city and its citizens as a whole and in a trans-scalar way.

Ludovico Quaroni once said to Solà-Morales, "There are two kinds of good architects, those who know how to observe and those who know how to produce. Do not fool yourself, no good architect has sought both." Knowing Solà-Morales, who was never easily satisfied, per se, I am sure that as soon as his mentor finished the

Fig. 5   Personal inscription for Manuel
de Solà-Morales from Jan Gehl
(Lorena Bello Gomez)

Fig. 6   Scheveningen Boulevard,
              The Hague, the Netherlands
              (Rosa Feliu)

Fig. 7   Scheveningen Boulevard,
              The Hague, the Netherlands
              (Rosa Feliu)

Scheveningen Boulevard,
The Hague, the Netherlands
(Rosa Feliu)

Fig. 8

sentence, he started to strategize how to overcome the challenge. In so doing, Solà-Morales founded the Laboratorio de Urbanismo de Barcelona for the study of the city as soon as he became full professor at the Escola Tècnica Superior d'Arquitectura de Barcelona (ESTAB) Department of Urban Planning in 1969, at the early age of thirty. By then, Solà-Morales already had a master of architecture degree from the ETSAB, a master of city planning from the Harvard Graduate School of Design where he studied with Josep Lluís Sert, a PhD from the ETSAB, and a degree in economics from the University of Barcelona. His career as an educator and researcher in academia flew always in parallel to his practice as a solo architect in his atelier, a beautiful old perfume factory in the upper slope of the Tibidabo, where many projects came to life and where I visited him many times when he became my PhD advisor.

To come to an end, knowing that he loved music and metaphors, I would say that Solà-Morales was a city choreographer. He was the orchestra director who would raise his hand to let society construct the city as a perfect artifact of inhabitation and collective imagination, with high standards of living. He described such a city as the "open city" and he helped its building by providing counterweights, always confronting the norm. He alerted us to the necessity of the collective and public when too much attention was placed on the private, or the other way around. He promoted urban capillarity with the introduction of porous membranes to overcome boundaries and limits in the city. He reclaimed difference as a counter to the homogeneity and sameness that globalization introduces to the contemporary city. More importantly,

Fig. 9   Scheveningen Boulevard,
               The Hague, the Netherlands
               (Rosa Feliu)

when every response to the city problems seemed to have become big or mega, Solà-Morales reminded us of the power of the small intervention—those gestures reached through acupunctural inserts with little cost and size, but with big effects. With the same principles, when all the world's analytical attention seemed invested in the flows and patterns of urbanization, Manuel de Solà-Morales outlined the power of a city corner as a synthetic act of urbanity that transcends culture, race, time, and geography. With his example, I hope that the Center for Advanced Urbanism will be able to keep that fantastic music going in the years to come.

Fig. 10   The Moll de la Fusta Wharf at the   opening (Salvador Sansuan, for
                 Barcelona 1992 Olympics Games   La Vanguardia)

Fig. 11   Manuel de Solà-Morales and
                            Ludovico Quaroni (Rosa Feliu)

Contributors

Stan Allen is an architect working in New York and the George Dutton '27 Professor of Architecture at Princeton University. From 2002 to 2012 he was Dean of the School of Architecture at Princeton. He holds degrees from Brown University, the Cooper Union and Princeton. His architectural firm, SAA/Stan Allen Architect, has realized buildings and urban projects in the United States, South America, and Asia. Responding to the complexity of the modern city in creative ways, Stan Allen has developed an extensive catalog of innovative design strategies, in particular looking at field theory, landscape architecture, and ecology as models to revitalize the practices of urban design. In 2008, he received a P/A Award for the Taichung Gateway Park and a Faith and Form Award for the CCV Chapel. In 2009 he received a P/A Award for the Yan-Ping Waterfront in Taipei, an AIA Award for the CCV Chapel, the John Q. Hejduk Award, and an Academy Award in Architecture from the American Academy of Arts and Letters; in 2010, his building for Paju Book City in South Korea received an AIA Award. In 2011, the Taichung InfoBox was recognized with a P/A Award, as well as AIA Awards from New York City, New York State and the Tri-State Region. In addition to numerous articles and project reviews, his architectural work is published in *Points + Lines: Diagrams and Projects for the City* (Princeton Architectural Press, 2001), and his essays in *Practice: Architecture, Technique, and Representation* (Routledge, 2008). His most recent book is the edited volume *Landform Building: Architecture's New Terrain* (Lars Müller, 2011).

Pierre Bélanger is a registered landscape architect and urban planner in Canada, the United States, and the Netherlands, and directs OPSYS. As an associate professor, he currently teaches graduate and postgraduate courses at the Harvard University Graduate School of Design, where his academic research and public work focus on the convergence of ecology and infrastructure in the interrelated fields of planning, design, and engineering. He is currently completing research for his forthcoming book entitled *Landscape Infrastructure: Urbanism beyond Engineering*, establishing a base discourse on the contemporary transformation of civil engineering, urban planning and landscape architecture. Bélanger completed a masters degree in landscape architecture at the Harvard Graduate School of Design and a PhD cum laude from Wageningen University. As a former project manager with Brinkman & Associates, Canada's largest reforestation and bioengineering contractor, Bélanger is a government-appointed member of the Ontario Food Terminal Board, recipient of the Professional Prix de Rome awarded by the Canada Council for the Arts and Special Adviser to the U.S. Army Corps of Engineers.

Lorena Bello Gomez teaches students fundamentals of the design of the built environment ranging from the scale of the object and buildings to that of the city and larger territories. She is also a doctoral candidate in urbanism at the Technical University of Catalonia (UPC). Lorena's research focuses on large-scale territorial implications of infrastructure and urbanization as catalysts for design. Her dissertation on this topic began under the guidance of the late Manuel de Solà-Morales and is concluding under Joan Busquets of the Harvard Graduate School of Design. She is also the founder of TERRALAB, in association with MIT's Center for Advanced Urbanism, to continue this research with projects in the United States and Europe.

Prior to 2008, Bello Gomez worked in Barcelona as project director at Aldayjover Architecture and Landscape where she led projects at different scales including those within the Water Park 2008 international exhibit in Zaragoza. She was also research assistant at the Joan Miró Foundation and the Building Tech Institute of Catalonia. Lorena holds a bachelor's and master's degree in architecture and civil engineering from the UPC where she graduated with honors, and a master of architecture in urban design from the Harvard Graduate School of Design.

Eran Ben-Joseph is professor and head of the Department of Urban Studies and Planning at MIT. His research and teaching areas include urban and physical design, standards and regulations, sustainable site planning technologies, and urban retrofitting. He has published numerous articles, monographs, and book chapters, and has authored and coauthored books. Prof. Ben-Joseph has worked as a city planner, urban designer, and landscape architect in Europe, Asia, the Middle East, and the United States, on projects including new towns, residential developments, streetscapes, stream restorations, and parks and recreation planning. He has led national and international multidisciplinary projects in Singapore, Barcelona, Santiago, Tokyo, and Washington, DC, among other places. Prof. Ben-Joseph is the recipient of the Wade Award for his work on *Representation of Places*, a collaborative project with MIT Media Lab, and the Milka Bliznakov Prize for his historical work "Pioneering Women of Landscape Architecture." He holds degrees from the University of California, Berkeley, and Chiba National University of Japan.

Don Briggs is the president of Federal Realty Boston. In this capacity, Briggs is responsible for managing Federal Realty Investment Trust's New England portfolio and for managing the trust's national pipeline of large-scale development. Briggs also serves as a member of the Trust's investment and executive committees. With over fifteen years experience in real estate development and the construction industry, he has been responsible for the development of several mixed use projects and public/ private endeavors, including the development of Rockville Town Square, phases of Bethesda Row, phases of Santana Row, and currently Assembly Square and Pike and Rose. Prior to joining Federal Realty in 2000, Briggs worked as a development manager for Cousins Properties and as a senior project manager with Whiting Turner Contracting Company. Briggs has a degree in architecture from the University of Florida. He currently serves as a board member for both National Association of Industrial and Office Properties (NAIOP) Massachusetts and A Better City and is on the advisory panel for the Urban Land Institute Boston.

Stephen Crosby has been the president of CSX Real Property Inc. since 2000. In this role, he is responsible for sales, leasing, and development of CSX properties.

Additionally, he oversees acquisition of property for railroad and industrial development, licensing of rail-corridor use by third parties, nonoperating property management, and corporate facilities management. His group is also responsible for the company's land records and fixed-asset agreements with other railroads, along with numerous other property-related responsibilities.

Crosby's tenure at CSX spans more than twenty-five years, affording comprehensive insight into the issues surrounding site identification, acquisition, and development. In addition to property-related duties, he serves on CSX Corporation's strategic development team and its pension investment committee.

Crosby earned his bachelor's degree from the University of Virginia and his master of business administration from the University of Florida. He has served as national chairman of NAIOP, and currently serves as a trustee of its Research Foundation and chairman of its investment committee. He has served as an advisory board member for the University of Virginia School of Architecture and as chairman of Downtown Vision, Inc., of Jacksonville, where he currently chairs its sustainability committee. He represents CSX on the Land Trust Alliance Corporate Council. He is a current member of the ULI North Florida Advisory Council, chairs its downtown committee, and also serves on the ULI's Public Development and Infrastructure National Council. He represents CSX on the board of the Delaware Otsego Corp. and the NYS&W Railroad.

Alexander D'Hooghe is associate professor with tenure at MIT and founding partner of the Organization for Permanent Modernity, a professional firm and think tank for urbanism and architecture with locations in Boston and Brussels. Currently, he also directs the Center for Advanced Urbanism at MIT, which focuses on large-scale contemporary design problems. He has published internationally, notably *The Liberal Monument* (Princeton Architectural Press, 2010) and recent papers in relevant journals in Germany, Israel, Spain, the Netherlands, Belgium, and the United States. His urban designs and analyses have included sites in New York City, Shenzhen, Brussels, Ostend, The Hague, Reykjavik, South Korea, and parts of Russia. With the design office, he develops durable architectures: simple artifacts able to handle complex demands and requirements. Ongoing projects include a masterplan for the slaughterhouse district in Brussels (including a 269,100 sq. ft. [25,000 sq. m] market building), development prototypes for middle ring suburbs in East Coast cities (for NAIOP), a series of public facilities and town centers around Brussels, a plan for the protection and expansion of the coastline between France and the Netherlands (42 miles [68 km], 2009), as well as a competition-winning entry for a large landfill in South Korea (155 sq. miles [401 sq. km], 2008). D'Hooghe obtained his PhD at the Berlage Institute in 2007 with TU Delft after receiving a master of urban design at the Harvard Graduate School of Design (GSD) in 2001 and a master of architecture and civil engineering from the University of Leuven in 1996. He has worked with, among others, Rem Koolhaas and Marcel Smets.

Jo Guldi is a historian of Britain and its empire. Her first book, *Roads to Power: Britain Invents the Infrastructure State* (Harvard, 2012), documents the rule of experts with the rise of the first national bureaucracy dedicated to the civilian connections that undergirded the Industrial Revolution and shows how battles over funding the roads divided the nation and caused strangers to stop speaking on the public street.

An assistant professor at Brown University, she has enjoyed fellowships from the Harvard Society of Fellows and the University of Chicago, where she has taught courses on landscape and capitalism since 1350. She has published on aspects of the spatial turn and interactions between strangers in London's public spaces. Her new project, *The Long Land War*, traces the global movement of land reform since 1860, when simultaneous famines and peasant riots in India, Ireland, and Scotland rocked the British Empire and caused the rethinking of property law among governing elites. In 2012–2013, she will be working on this project while finishing her stead at the Society of Fellows, visiting archives in the United Kingdom, India, and North America. Guldi is also involved in conversations about digital technology and how it affects pedagogy, publishing, and research among historians. She has published several articles about digital methods for creating knowledge from the new mass-digitized databases online.

Guldi has written for *Counterpunch* and the *Huffington Post* on issues of the politics of landscape, and she maintains a blog at http://landscape.blogspot.com.

Alex Klatskin is a general partner of Forsgate Industrial Partners, a private industrial real estate development and investment firm based in Teterboro, New Jersey that has built and owns ten million square feet of industrial property. Before joining Forsgate in 1992, Klatskin was with the New York City architectural firm Kohn Pedersen Fox Associates, working on commercial projects in London and New York.

Klatskin was the 2011 national chairman of NAIOP. At NAIOP, he is also a former president of the New Jersey chapter. In addition, Alex is a member of the Washington, DC–based Real Estate Roundtable, the Board of Regents of the American Architectural Foundation, the College of Fellows of the American Institute of Architects, the Architectural League of New York, and the American Real Estate Society.

He has been a visiting architectural critic at the University of Michigan, the University of Illinois, Florida A&M, Catholic University, and the Illinois Institute of Technology. He has been a visiting lecturer in the real estate programs at Cornell and Johns Hopkins as well as the School of Architecture and Planning at MIT.

Klatskin holds a bachelor of science from the University of Illinois and a master of architecture from the University of Maryland. He is a registered architect in New York, New Jersey, and the District of Columbia and a licensed professional planner in New Jersey. He lives in New York City with his wife and their two children.

Christopher Lee is the cofounder and principal of Serie Architects based in London, Mumbai, and Beijing. He is adjunct associate professor of urban design at the GSD, where he previously served as design critic in 2011–2012. Prior to that he was the director of the Architecture Association (AA) Projective Cities MPhil program (2010–2012) as well as AA diploma and intermediate unit master (2002–2009). Lee graduated with the AA Diploma (honors), received the RIBA President's Medal Commendation Award, and received his PhD in architecture and urbanism from the Berlage Institute and Delft University of Technology.

The work of Serie is underpinned by the exploration of the problem of type and the city, with particular focus on the renewed relevance of typological reasoning and experimentation—or working projectively in series—to describe, conceptualize, theorize, and ultimately project new typological ideas for and from the city. Serie is the recipient of the prestigious BD Young Architect of the Year Award, was recently named as one of the ten visionary architects for the new decade by the Leading European Architects Forum, and was selected by ICON as one of twenty essential young architects in the world in 2008. Serie's current projects include the Singapore Subordinate Courts Complex, BMW London 2012 Pavilion, and Wuxi Xishan Civic Complex, China.

Lee has authored and edited publications, and he lectures widely. The work of Serie has been exhibited as a traveling solo exhibition.

Robert Levit is professor and director of the master of architecture program at the University of Toronto John H. Daniels Faculty of Architecture, Landscape, and Design. Levit joined Daniels in January of 2002 and was director of the master of urban design program from 2003 to 2010. He is a partner in the design firm Khoury Levit Fong and has won several international architecture and urban design competitions. He is currently designing the research district for a new satellite city in Tai Yuan, Shanxi province, China. His work links the urban and architectural scales. He has led research funded by the province of Ontario examining the relationship between density and urban form and providing models for urban intensification. His work on housing types has received academic and professional awards, and his design work and writing on architecture have appeared in numerous domestic and foreign publications. Levit teaches in both the urban design and architecture programs of the Faculty. He holds a master's degree in architecture from Harvard University, and received his bachelor of arts degree from Columbia University. Prior to beginning his own practice he worked for the Portuguese architect Alvaro Siza.

Petra Todorovich Messick is senior officer of outreach and communications in the Northeast Corridor Infrastructure Investment Development (NEC IID) division at Amtrak. NEC IID is the new business line at Amtrak devoted to planning, maintaining, and improving the Northeast Corridor—the rail corridor stretching from Boston to Washington, DC—and hosting more than two thousand daily intercity, commuter, and freight trains. In her position at Amtrak, she conducts strategic outreach to a range of partners and stakeholders impacted by Amtrak's plans for the corridor.

Prior to coming to Amtrak, Messick was director of America 2050, the Regional Plan Association's national infrastructure planning and policy program, which provides leadership on a broad range of transportation, sustainability, and economic development issues impacting America's growth in the twenty-first century. Prior to the launch of America 2050, Messick directed RPA's Region's Core program and coordinated the Civic Alliance to Rebuild Downtown New York, a network of organizations that came together shortly after 9/11 to promote the rebuilding of the World Trade Center site and Lower Manhattan.

Messick is also an assistant visiting professor at the Pratt Institute, where her teaching focuses on implementing plans and projects in dynamic, politically fragmented metropolitan regions. Messick received a BA from Vassar College and a master of city and regional planning from Rutgers University.

James Oberstar was born on September 10, 1934 in Chisholm, Minnesota. His father, Louis Oberstar, was an iron ore miner, and his mother, Mary, worked in a garment factory to supplement the family income while she raised him and his two brothers.

In college, Oberstar worked in the open pit mines to pay for his education. He graduated summa cum laude with a double major in French and political science from the College of St. Thomas in St. Paul, Minnesota, in 1956. He continued his education at the College of Europe in Bruges, Belgium, Laval University in Quebec, and Georgetown University in Washington. From 1959 to 1962 he worked at the US naval mission to Haiti, teaching French and Creole to US Marine Corps personnel and English to Haitian military.

In 1963, Oberstar began working for Rep. John Blatnik from Minnesota's eighth congressional district. When Rep. Blatnik retired in 1974, Oberstar sought and won his first term in the House of Representatives. The people of northeast Minnesota returned him to Washington for seventeen more terms; he ended his career as the longest-serving member of Congress in Minnesota's history.

In the thirty-six years he served in the House, Congressman Oberstar became the body's leading expert on transportation policy. He was a champion of safety in all modes of travel and a fierce advocate for federal investment in our national transportation infrastructure.

Henk W. J. Ovink is principal of Rebuild by Design (RBD) and senior advisor for Secretary Shaun Donovan of the US Department of Housing and Urban Development and the Hurricane Sandy Rebuilding Task Force. He leads the long-term and innovation rebuilding efforts for Secretary Donovan. Ovink started, developed, and leads the RBD competition. RBD was developed to ignite innovation for a new standard of regional resilience in design and development, in building and rebuilding in the light of climate change, sea level rise, and future economic, ecological, and cultural demands. RBD was named number one in CNN's 2013 list of the top ten most innovative ideas.

Ovink was both director general of spatial planning and water affairs and direc-tor of national spatial planning for the Kingdom of the Netherlands. Ovink teaches at Harvard GSD, UCLA Architecture & Urban Design, Columbia Graduate School of Architecture, Planning, and Preservation, Syracuse University School of Architecture, Delft University of Technology, and the University of Groningen. He is a member of the advisory boards for MIT's Center for Advanced Urbanism, the Berlage Institute, the Delft University of Technology Faculty of Architecture, and the Master City Developer Rotterdam, and he is chair of the research program on Strong Cities. Ovink is a mem-ber of the Urban Age Program within the London School of Economics Cities. He was curator for the fifth International Architecture Biennale Rotterdam 2012 "Making City" and curates the debate series "Design and Politics: The Next Phase" for Aedes Network Campus Berlin. Ovink initiated the research program Design and Politics, is the connecting chair of Design and Politics at Delft University of Technology, and is chief editor for the series of publications with 010 Publishers called *Design and Politics*.

Stephen J. Ramos is assistant professor in the College of Environment and Design at the University of Georgia. His research explores the roles and meanings of large-scale infrastructure in shaping port geographies. He is author of *Dubai Amplified: The Engineering of a Port Geography* (Ashgate Press, 2010), and coeditor of *Infrastructure Sustainability and Design* (Routledge, 2012). He is a founding editor of the journal *New Geographies* and editor-in-chief of *New Geographies 1: After Zero* (Harvard GSD and University Press, 2009). His writing has appeared in *Harvard Design Magazine, Volume,* and *Neutra*. He recently curated "Discrete Aperture: The Work of Nils Folke Anderson" at the University of Georgia Circle Gallery as part of a yearlong series on Art + Infrastructure. His professional practice includes work with the Fundación Metrópoli in Madrid and the International Society of City and Regional Planners in The Hague, along with NGO work throughout Latin America. He received his doctor of design degree from the Harvard Graduate School of Design.

Adèle Naudé Santos, FAIA, was appointed dean of MIT School of Architecture + Planning in February of 2004. Prior to that, she was professor at the University of California, Berkeley, where her academic focus was the design of housing envi-ronments. Her academic career includes professorships at University of California, Berkeley, Harvard University, Rice University, and the University of Pennsylvania, where she also served as chair of the Department of Architecture. She was the founding dean of the new School of Architecture at University of California, San Diego, and has had numerous visiting appointments around the world.

In addition to her administrative duties, Dean Santos and fellow MIT faculty and students have begun a research project with a major firm in China to design and construct a demonstration business park. She is principal architect In the San Francisco–based firm, Santos Prescott and Associates. Her architectural and planning projects include affordable and luxury housing and institutional buildings throughout the globe. She is currently working on projects in California, Guatemala, and China. Dean Santos has received many housing awards and honors including the 2009 Topaz Medallion for Excellence in Architectural Education. She also serves as a juror for numerous national and international design competitions and award programs.

Dean Santos has an AA Diploma from the Architectural Association in London, an MArch in urban design from Harvard University, and an MArch and master of city planning from the University of Pennsylvania.

Roger Sherman founded Roger Sherman Architecture and Urban Design (RSAUD) in 1989. He has personally been the recipient of many honors and awards, including being a finalist for the Ventulette Distinguished Chair in Architectural Design at Georgia Tech in 2004, presenting a paper at the pragmatism conference at the Museum of Modern Art in New York in 2000, being a Wheelwright fellow at Harvard in 1995, and a Skidmore, Owings & Merrill traveling fellow in 1984. In 1987, he and Edmund Chang earned the commission for the West Hollywood Civic Center by virtue of having won an international design competition from a field of over three hundred entrants.

Sherman currently serves on the board of directors of the Westside Urban Forum (WUF) and on the advisory board of Livable Places, a nonprofit developer of affordable housing. He has also served on the city of West Hollywood's Cultural Heritage Advisory Board and as a partner of the Weingart Center Association, a homeless organization. Sherman is an adjunct associate professor at UCLA's Department of Architecture and Urban Design, and he was formerly director of the FreshURBS postgraduate program at the Southern California Institute of Architecture (SCI-Arc). He was a visiting studio professor at Harvard GSD in 2001 and has both lectured and served as a visiting critic at a wide range of academic institutions, including Yale, Rice, Princeton, Michigan, Arizona State, and CCAC. His work and writing are widely published.

Marcel Smets has studied architecture at the University of Ghent in 1970 and urban design at TU Delft in 1974. He obtained a PhD from the University of Leuven (1976), where he was appointed as the chair of urbanism in 1978. He has been active in theory and history with books on H. Hoste, Charles Buls, the Belgian garden cities, and the reconstruction of Belgium after 1914. He served as a critic for *Archis*, *Topos*, *Lotus*, and *Casabella*, and as juror for many competitions. He was founding member of the International Laboratory of Architecture and Urban Design (Urbino 1978), visiting professor at the University of Thessaloniki (1987), and design critic at Harvard GSD (2002, 2003, 2004). From 1989 to 2001, he founded and directed Projectteam Stadsontwerp, a research and design group of the University of Leuven, specialized in the urban reappropriation of abandoned industrial areas and outworn infrastructures. In this position, he acted as chief urban designer for widely published conversion projects in Leuven, Antwerp, and Hoeilaart in Belgium, Rouen in France, and Genoa and Conegliano in Italy. In June 2005, Smets was appointed chief architect for the Flemish region, a five-year mandate in which he managed the public design commissions for the government. In line with his design practice, Smets's main research interest shifted to infrastructure as a means of structuring cities and landscapes. In 2010, he coauthored with K. Shannon the influential book *The Landscape of Contemporary Infrastructure* (010 Publishers, 2010). Today, he chairs the Scientific and Steering Committee for the City on the Move Institute (IVM), and leads the urban design team in charge of transforming the Isle of Nantes.

Malcolm Smith is the founding design director of the Integrated Urbanism Unit at Arup in London and the Arup global leader of masterplanning and urban design. He joined Arup after completing his master's degree in architecture at Yale University. Prior to undertaking his master's, Malcolm worked in Australia on a wide range of projects including waterfront development, tertiary education buildings and master-plans, entertainment, and arts facilities.

Malcolm sets the design strategy for a wide range of urban design projects, both in the United Kingdom and internationally, that have sustainable placemaking at their core. Besides the physical issues of places, his work encompasses issues such as integrated systems, resource efficiency, cultural strategy, risk and resilience. This approach comes together in the process of "integrated urbanism."

Besides his project work, Malcolm has been an invited member of the Commission for Architecture and the Built Environment (CABE). He is invited to lecture around the world on sustainable environments, most recently at the Green Building Council of Australia, Melbourne, and the Prince's Foundation in the United Kingdom. He was an invited participant at the inaugural Global Humanitarian Forum in Geneva and an invited advisor to the Gore Foundation. He is appointed by the City of Amsterdam as lead designer for Zuidas, the new commercial center for Amsterdam.

Nader Tehrani is professor and head of the Department of Architecture at the MIT School of Architecture + Planning. He is also principal and founder of NADAAA, a practice dedicated to the advancement of design innovation, interdisciplinary collaboration, and an intensive dialogue with the construction industry.

Previously, Tehrani was principal and founder of Office dA (1986–2011), where he designed award-winning projects such as Tongxian Art Gatehouse in Beijing, Fleet Library at Rhode Island School of Design, the LEED-certified Helios House in Los Angeles, the Interfaith Spiritual Center at Northeastern University, Banq restaurant, and the LEED Gold–certified Macallen Building in Boston. Examining spaces of pedagogy, Tehrani recently completed the renovation of the Hinman Building at the Georgia Institute of Technology and is currently redesigning schools of architecture at the University of Melbourne and the University of Toronto.

Tehrani's research and installations have been exhibited in notable venues, he has authored several articles, and his work has been internationally reviewed and published.

Cino Zucchi, born in Milan in 1955, earned a BSAD at MIT in 1978 and a laurea in architettura at the Politecnico di Milano in 1979, where he is professor and chair of architectural and urban design and a member of the PhD program. He served as visiting professor in housing and urbanization at the Harvard Graduate School of Design, and he is regularly invited to give lectures and sit on architectural juries both in Italy and abroad.

He is author of the books *L'Architettura dei Cortili Milanesi 1535–1706* (Asnago e Vender), *Architetture e Progetti 1925–1970* (Cino Zucchi), and *Inspiration and Process in Architecture*, as well as editor of the book *Bau-Kunst-Bau*. He participated in the organization and exhibition design of the fifteenth, sixteenth, eighteenth, and nineteenth Triennales of Milan, is on the scientific committee of the twenty-first Triennale of Milan, and is curator of the Italian Pavilion at the fourteenth Venice Biennale.

Together with his studio CZA, he has designed and realized many commercial, residential, and public buildings, public spaces, masterplans, and renewals of industrial, agricultural, and historical areas, and he has participated and won numerous competitions nationally and internationally. Relevant accomplishments are the renewals of the former industrial areas of Junghans in Venice and Portello in Milan. Recent works include the Keski Pasila masterplan in Helsinki, the Group M office building in Assago (Milan), the Salewa Headquarters in Bozen, residential complexes in Milan, Parma, Ravenna, and Bologna, the new Lavazza headquarters, and the extension of the National Automobile Museum in Turin, which won the In/Arch-ANCE 2011 award for architecture. www.zucchiarchitetti.com